D0844050

500 DAYS

TO THE LUNA
FAMILY!!!

500 DAYS

What I Learned From The Moment
That Changed Everything

STEVE ZAKUANI

KINGDOM
HOPE

© 2014 by Steve Zakuani

All rights reserved. No part of this book may be reproduced or transmitted in any form or by any means whatsoever, including photocopying, recording or by any information storage and retrieval system, without written permission from the publisher except in the case of brief quotations embodied in critical articles and reviews. For more information contact 17837 1ˢᵗ Avenue South #106 Normandy Park, WA 98148.

Grateful acknowledgment for permission to reprint images in this book is made to: Rod Mar (front cover image) Anthony Thurston (Back Cover Image)

Laurie Hodges, Jane Gershovich and Mike Russell (Interior Images). Thank you for capturing some of the most meaningful moments of my life.

A massive thank you to the following contributors who have worked on this project; your time, effort, and dedication are forever appreciated:

Cover design by David Taylor of Sugarsled Creative
Editorial work by Scott Parker of Hawthorne Books
Interior design by Inkwater Press
Website and social media by Stephen Reed of Stevonselects
www.500DaysBook.com
www.kingdom-hope.org

ISBN 978-0-9862510-0-9

First Paperback Edition

2 3 4 5 6 7 8 9 10

DEDICATION

This book is for anyone who has ever been to rock bottom. I hope this story will inspire you to keep on fighting.

This book is for every fan who supported me during my career, through the good times and the bad. Your support, your cheers, and words of encouragement, gave me strength to keep going even when I wanted to give up. I also thank you all for supporting this self-publishing effort with your generous donations through my Kickstarter campaign. Special thanks to Ryan Snyder for your generous show of support.

SPECIAL DEDICATION

As you read this book you will see the name Myles Munroe show up throughout my story. He was my mentor, a father figure, and a great source of inspiration to me over the years. He passed away as I was finalizing this book and so I dedicate the finished product to his memory.

NOTES

In the United Kingdom, where I grew up and went to school, some words are spelled slightly differently than how they are in the United States. Because this book is primarily intended for an American market, I've ignored everything my teachers taught me and have adopted the American spellings of any words that are different in British English. I've also tried to use American terms and metaphors as opposed to British ones. However, one thing I wasn't able to do was to use the word soccer instead of football. My English friends would never have forgiven me. So, as you read about my experiences in football, I am talking about soccer, not American football.

CONTENTS

FOREWORD
by Sigi Schmid

I t was a rainy cool evening in Columbus Ohio. The date was November 7, 2008. I was going to the soccer stadium to watch Ohio St. play the ranked men's soccer team from the University of Akron. I was going to see Steve Zakuani primarily, although Akron had a lot of good players. I had been watching Steve since his first year in 2007 at Akron. I had driven to Akron many times in 2007 and 2008 to see him play. Part of college scouting for the Columbus Crew who I worked for at the time as the head coach. I settled into a seat in the stands made sure I was warm and waited for the game to begin.

I knew Steve was a good player he had shown that many times in the games I saw him play. His speed, dribbling ability and that deceptive first step. However, to make it at the next level, the pro level you need something extra, skill alone does not do it. At times the collegiate game was too easy for him. He took some breaks, did he have the character, the will and drive to be a pro?

Twelve minutes in Steve scored, and that score stood until halftime. *Would it be another easy game for Akron? Would I see something special tonight?* I was not sure. In the 48th and the 49th minute Ohio State scored and suddenly momentum had swung and the game was in the balance.

Zakuani exerted himself and set up Ben Zemanski for the tying goal. But less than a minute later Ohio State scored to retake the lead.

Then it happened, I saw this talented player take his team on his back and drive them to victory. Steve scored the tying goal in the 68th minute and then beat a couple of players in the 82nd minute to provide the assist for a Blair Gavin winning goal. Akron had won 4-3. Steve Zakuani had scored 2 goals and gotten 2 assists. It was this game that convinced me of his drive and will power and that was when I knew he could be a difference maker.

January 15, 2009 I was in Saint Louis at the MLS draft. Now I was the coach of the Seattle Sounders FC and we had the number one pick in the draft. *Who would that be?* Steve Zakuani did not have a good combine in Florida. I had sung his praises to my new boss Adrian Hanauer, and our technical director Chris Henderson. They were not sure based upon his performances at the combine. But I remembered that night in Columbus and knew what he had. We all spoke, at the end we all agreed to take Steve with our number one pick. There could have been safer picks, but you only get so many chances to draft a player with special talents and gifts. I told Adrian he could be a big star or a bust, there would be no in between. We drafted Steve and the journey began.

The first year was a whirlwind. It was our first year in the league as an expansion team. Everyone was uncertain as to how we would do. I felt if we got some confidence early we would be alright. We had some talent and some workers. It was a good mix and the feeling on the field and the locker room was good. I was deciding how and when to use Steve. He had the talent and we needed his ability to unbalance a defense with his dribbling on the field. He was also a better passer than I had realized when watching him play. But working hard every day and being challenged every day at training was a concept he was still adjusting to. We had some guys like Evans, LeToux, Scott and others who worked hard all the time and set a high standard. Steve was reaching for that daily.

Our first ever game was at home in Seattle against New York. Great crowd and most expected us to lose. We won 3-0 and Zakuani came on as a sub. He was very sharp. The next week I started him and he got his first assist. He took on Beltran, faked in, then out, then in again, pass to Jaqua, goal. He started again in our first road game in Toronto and scored his first goal for the club. The talent was there and he was improving daily on his training approach. He was on his way to being a key member for our team.

In 2009 he averaged 69 minutes a game but was often upset with me when I pulled him out of games. But I had to, his fitness was not there yet. When you have talented players who are so skillful, they can get away with less effort at training. I was working on adding that work to his skill level. We bumped heads at times but in the end he worked harder and got more minutes. It was the start for Steve of understanding that he had to work to be better than the rest.

It was not a lot of fun at training to be the right back who played against Steve on a daily basis. He could tear you apart. James Riley improved going against Zakuani daily. But as a coach and coaching staff we would marvel at some of the things he could do. It was brilliant. The frustration only came in because our expectations kept growing but Steve was on a good path. His innate dribbling ability and the speed at which he could perform you cannot teach, he was an incredible talent.

Year two was something we were all looking forward to. There was a little more pressure in the club due to our success in year one. An Open Cup title and the playoffs in year one were measuring sticks now. The pressure on the individual players was also increased. That included Steve. *Would Zakuani be better than in year one? Was he going to be fitter? Would the opponent have figured him out? Steve had finished year one with 4 goals and 4 assists. Would year 2 be better?*

Steve Zakuani finished year 2 with eleven goals and 6 assists. Twice he had the goal of the week, and was voted league player of the week twice. On top of that he averaged almost 79 minutes a game, ten more than the year before. Steve had worked harder in the offseason than ever before. It was a big improvement but he could still do more. But remember for a wide player to get a goal every three games is fantastic. Opponents started to game plan for Steve. They started dropping wide midfielders to double on him. So I started to move him around a bit more. Switching wings going into the middle a bit more so the opponent had a harder time keeping track of him.

Steve can be stubborn at times and we would have some disagreements. I know I can be stubborn as well. But our understanding was good and in the end we respected each other and knew that we wanted the best for the team. The team and its success was important to Steve. But like all creative players he needed a little bit of space. Finding the right balance was an ongoing process.

By the end of year two Steve had established himself as one of the top attacking talents in the league. We would talk about whether he could represent the USA one day, or would it be for his native country the Congo in Africa? The third year was going to be the year that he could emerge as a star in our league. He worked even harder in the offseason and his training approach was definitely improving and it was making him a better player. He wanted to have success, but he also wanted more than just an Open Cup title which we had won again in year two.

The club entered year three with a lot of optimism. We had a good group of players and we had guys with star potential. Steve was one of those guys. *How much could he shoulder this year?* He had a great relationship with Randy Noteboom our trainer and would work hard with him on maintenance issues and preparing for training and games. He had a love hate relationship with our fitness coach Dave Tenney, but it had become more love and he saw the good it was doing for him. He was stronger and fitter as he entered his third season. I was pleased with how he had grown.

Steve was now playing full games. His fitness had improved and I did not sub him out. The team got off to a bad start. We lost our first two but then we tied our next two, then won and then came the game in Colorado. Steve had missed game two in New York due to illness. In our next three games he had a goal or an assist in each game. You could see his confidence grow and the team starting to rely on him when things were on the line. His numbers were projecting to take another jump in year three and his minutes would be up again.

The game in Colorado was important to our team as we were working out of our early season slump. It started like any other game. The tackle and the resulting aftermath are a bit of blur in my mind. It had happened right in front of their bench and 20-30 yards from our bench. But right away we knew it was serious. We heard it and saw it. My assistant Brian Schmetzer was on our trainer to get over there right away. As the head coach I knew we had to sub so I tried to get that player, Flaco Fernandez up and warming up. After a lengthy time they had Steve on a stretcher and started taking him off the field. Everyone tried to offer a word of encouragement or just touch his hand or the stretcher as it went by. The players were in shock. How we won that game I will never knew. We seemed to play the rest of the game in a daze. We talked about winning for Steve at halftime but it all seemed so unreal.

After the game I just wanted to know where Steve was and could we get to him? The club was fantastic and some of us stayed behind in Denver to be with Steve. Randy Noteboom our trainer was great and Adrian Hanauer eventually flew Steve back on his private jet once the surgeries were done. But we knew he was out for the season and we hoped he would play again. Early on that was not certain.

The following weeks had surgeries for Steve, getting his family over from Europe and just trying to help him with all the immediate needs. As a team we had to continue but it was difficult for all knowing we had lost such a key player.

Rehab was in the distant future. Compartment syndrome was an issue and more surgeries then I can count. Eventually Steve was able to return to the training center and start on the road back. The players and staff were all supportive and we talked about a plan of recovery. Our trainer and fitness coach took the lead. I could sense his frustration at times, but we all knew there was no other way.

Going into the following season Steve was making physical progress but the mental side also had to be overcome. Running and doing all those things are sometimes the easy part. Knowing whether you can take a hit, still have that burst and instinct is another thing. Steve was improving but it was often two steps forward and then one back. Not easy.

As a coach as he got closer to playing I was starting to consider what would be the process. Our fans were great and missed Steve. *How and when should I bring him back?* That was something I talked to Steve about, yet eventually I would have to decide.

Keeping Steve motivated was hard at times and easy at other times. To go through what he went through and try to get back to your peak is a tough process. Sometimes I thought he looked ready but he did not feel that way, so we had to put on the breaks. It was frustrating for the coaches but it was more frustrating for Steve.

Finally I thought the time had come. We were going to play Colorado at home. Steve was a little uncertain but I thought we needed to do this. Playing against the team that this injury happened against and the player would help us all put this behind us. There was a clarity that I hoped this could bring. I named Steve to the subs bench. After half-time he warmed up with the rest of the reserves. The crowd got electric and you could feel the anticipation. I called Steve over to bring him on. Then Colorado scored to make it a one goal game and I thought about changing my mind. I am glad I did not. When the change was announced the roar was unbelievable. The return had finally happened and it was a great feeling. The date was July 7, 2012. September 2, 2012 he started his first game versus Dallas.

It was a long journey. I am honored and humbled to write this intro for Steve. Adversity defines character and he certainly has dealt with more adversity than anyone should have to go through. This book is about character, enjoy the read, feel the journey.

SIGI SCHMID
December 2014

CHAPTER 1
THE WORST MOMENT

You'll never find a better sparring partner than adversity.

—GOLDA MEIR

DENVER, COLORADO
APRIL 2011

The pain is unbearable. This is bad, really bad. I keep replaying the sequence of events in my head:

I call for the ball.
I receive it.
I control it.
I turn with it.
I begin to dribble it up the pitch.
And then it happens.
BANG! I feel the tackle come in.
From this moment on my entire career will hang in the balance.

My leg goes numb as I fall and land on my back. I look up at my leg; it's pointing in two different directions. That can't be good. Legs aren't supposed to do that. My leg is bent the wrong way. That can't be good at all. There are a few thousand people in the stadium, but all I hear is silence. I feel like the world has stopped spinning. Numb, tingling sensations race up and down my leg. Teammates rush to my side along with a couple of doctors and team trainers.

"What do you feel?"

"Do you remember what happened?"

"Where is the pain?"

I'm being asked a lot of questions; too many questions for my liking. Just get me to a hospital, my leg is killing me. There will be time for questions later. Right now all I know is that something terrible has happened to me and that my leg hurts like hell.

I take a closer look at my surroundings and my stomach sinks even more as I begin to realize that I may have underestimated the severity of what had just happened to me. I can see the players on the Colorado Rapids bench with their hands over their mouths. We are opponents during the game, but when something like what just happened happens football has to take a backseat. More than a few players are saying prayers for me. The collective look of disbelief I see on the faces of everyone I make eye contact with not only gives me the chills but also serves as added confirmation that I've likely suffered an injury far worse than anything anyone in this stadium has ever seen before. I lay my head back on the grass and close my eyes. *My season is over, and maybe even my career.* It's a scary thought. *I can't think like that, I need to stay positive.* I take a deep breath and compose myself.

As I'm lying on the grass, a nasty battle begins to take place within me. On the one hand, I fight to remain positive as I tell myself that I'll get through this, but on the other, a small voice fires back, "Get through this? Did you not see how your leg was bent in the wrong direction? It's over." I try to shut that side of me up but it proves to be impossible. The fear that it may all be over is very real. I try to look on the bright side: I'm young and I've bounced back from hardships before. This fight between keeping hope and giving in would continue for the next three years as I dealt with the physical and mental ramifications of what took place April 22, 2011.

Most professional athletes don't like to think of the day that their careers will end. We don't like to think of a life without the sports we love, the sports we have given so much to and have received so much from. At some level we all find our identity in what we do. The field, the pitch, the court, and the arena have been our sanctuaries and our escapes from our troubles. Ask most athletes to describe what it feels like to be out on the field or the court and you will hear them say things like:

- I feel free.
- I feel alive.
- It's the only time I come to life.
- It's exhilarating.

I've also used some of those same responses when I've been asked questions along those lines in the past because they're true; there's just something invigorating about being gifted enough at a sport that you can turn it from simply being a passion or a hobby into a career. To get paid for doing something you've loved and have done since you were a young kid is a pretty good deal. To have people know who you are because of what you do, and to receive a lot of praise for what you once did when no one was even watching, is an amazing thing. We would do it forever if we could because it's a great, secure way to earn a living. And that's probably why we try to never think of, or imagine, a life in which we no longer play a sport for a living.

But deep down, way down, we all know that it has to end one day. We just never want to think of that one day because it's extremely uncomfortable to do so; and for now at least, it seems so far off in the future that we don't need to think about it. We know that eventually we will have to find a new identity, a new passion, and a new way of making a living that doesn't include playing the sport we love, but right now, in this very moment, we want to keep on feeling alive, we want to keep feeling free, and we want to keep experiencing that exhilarating feeling that playing our sport gives us. I'm all for that, and I've always been that way.

But what happens when the future is dragged into your present? What happens when one day is no longer ten years away but today? What do you do when life forces you to picture an immediate future that doesn't include playing your sport for a living? It's a different ball game when you no longer have the option or luxury of pushing thoughts of life after football, basketball, baseball or whatever sport you play, off into the future. When the instant reality of a life without this thing in which so much of your identity and happiness has been generated from confronts you, a million unwelcome questions can race through your mind.

- How will I make a living?
- What will I do with my time?
- Am I even good at anything else?

It's one thing to have to face those questions when you are thirty-five and have had a long career. At that age you know you are in the final days of your career as an athlete and you can mentally make peace with the end because you know it's coming. It's an entirely different thing, however, to have to face those same questions when you are only twenty-three and are about to enter the prime years of your career. At twenty-three you are just getting started and you shouldn't have to envision the end. No twenty-three-year-old athlete should have to entertain the thought of his or her career being over, but that's the position I found myself in after April 22, 2011. At the age of twenty-three, thoughts of retirement began to enter my mind, and it would be an ongoing fight to push them aside from that moment onward.

Coming off the 2010 Major League Soccer season, I was feeling good. My team, the Seattle Sounders FC, had made the playoffs for the second year running, we had retained the US Open Cup, I had scored eleven goals, and people were giving me a lot of praise for the way I played the game.

All of our best players would be returning for the following season, and under the leadership of our coach, Sigi Schmid, we were only going to get better. That offseason I spent some time training with Everton, one of the top teams in England, and I played an exhibition game for my birth country, the Democratic Republic of Congo, which was an amazing experience. It's because of all of these factors that I entered the 2011 season with a feeling that I was primed to become one of the best players in our entire league and that eventually my performances would catch the attention of a good team in Europe that would want to sign me.

I had been playing football for eighteen years at that point, professionally for two of them, and I had never felt as confident in my abilities as I did heading into my third professional season. This was my mind frame as I prepared for the sixth game of that season on a Friday night in Denver, Colorado, on April 22, 2011.

As a team, we hadn't made the best of starts to the season, as we had won only one game, tied two, and lost the other two. In spite of our slow start we felt as if we were turning the corner after winning our previous game against the Chicago Fire, a game in which I scored the winning goal. On a personal level, I felt great and was playing very well. I already had two goals and a couple of assists, but beyond the stats I was just really enjoying my football. I've never been a big stats guy; playing well and enjoying what I'm doing has always been the thing that drives me. It's a lot easier to enjoy playing football, and to win, when you're playing well, so I have always tried to just focus on playing well in the next game and expected the wins and stats to be a byproduct of that. The next game for me to focus on playing well in was against the Colorado Rapids.

Now, if you would have told me before the game that in the coming days I would have to contemplate retirement, a life without football, doing something else, and never playing again, I simply wouldn't have believed you, because I couldn't foresee a circumstance in which that would have to be the case. I never anticipated suffering an injury so severe that it made that abstract possibility become a very real one. There was no way I could have seen it coming. It really did hit me like a ton of bricks.

To followers of MLS, the story is well known. In the third minute of the game against Colorado I received the ball and as I turned to dribble it up the pitch a really strong tackle to my right leg stopped me in my tracks. My leg was broken—both my tibia and fibula. I would find out the next day after surgery that I had also developed something called compartment syndrome, which basically meant that I had suffered some severe nerve damage that required me to have another surgery. If I didn't have this second surgery I risked losing the nerve function in my right foot. That was a scary proposition because once nerve function is gone it's next to impossible to get back. Being who I was, a footballer, and doing what I did for a living, playing football, losing feeling in my foot was the worst possible thing that could happen to me.

In the days and weeks that followed I had the doctors tell me that I would definitely walk again and that I would regain some level of function in my right leg, but they always stopped short of reassuring me that I would ever play again. They couldn't assure me of that because they weren't sure how well I would heal, and they also weren't sure how much irreversible damage had been done to the nerves that control the sensation in my right foot. A broken leg and compartment syndrome, it was one of the worst injuries ever seen in our sport. I've been told that YouTube clips relating to this incident have over 700,000 combined views. They probably have more by now, but I wouldn't know because I've never watched them.

In the months that followed the injury I would be asked a

thousand times by well meaning fans and supporters when I expected
to be back. I often told them that I'd be back soon and I really believed
that I would. However, if I may be transparent, I have to tell you that
my confidence and determination to get back on the field would sometimes give way to questions of what if:

- What if I never play again? What will I do with my life?
- What if my leg never heals to be how it was before? Will I ever
  be the player I could have been?
- What if I have played my last professional game?

These were extremely uncomfortable questions that no athlete should
ever have to deal with, and even less so if that athlete is only twenty-three
years old and playing the best football of his career at the time.

I learned a lot from my injury. The main thing I learned was that it is
important to always have a positive attitude and outlook no matter
how bad things get. I learned that in life nothing is permanent or guaranteed, so the best way to manage hardships and negative changes is to
realize that they are a normal part of life, they happen to everyone, and
that they can only defeat you if you allow them to. In other words: it's
not what happens to you, it's how you respond to what happens to you,
that determines victory or defeat when facing challenges and hardships.

Another thing I learned was that every thing that happens in life
can be a learning experience if we allow it to be. One of the great things
about life is that it's an ongoing journey that offers us countless opportunities to learn about ourselves, about other people, and about the
world around us. Tragedies, challenges, obstacles, storms, hardships,
tough times—whatever you want to call them—are the times in which
we often have the opportunity to learn the most about ourselves. I
wish tragedy on no one, but if such a thing occurs, my advice is to use
it as a learning tool, to use it as a chance to look inside yourself and
figure out things about you that you didn't know before. I guarantee
that you will learn incredible things about your potential, your resil-
ience, and your inner strength.

I learned that I was a lot stronger mentally than I'd ever thought
I was. I also learned that having a positive outlook doesn't mean that

you never have any doubts, fears, or moments in which you just want to vent. I learned that it is normal to wrestle with doubts and difficult questions when you feel wronged or hard done by life. I also learned that sometimes it's okay to accept that there are no clear answers as to why something bad happens to you. Sometimes that's just the way life goes; things happen.

I learned that forgiveness is one of the greatest gifts you can give yourself. I never held any bitterness toward the person who injured me, and I still don't. I reached out to him some time after the injury, and I exchanged jerseys with him the next time I played against him to show that there were no hard feelings. The jersey exchange actually took place in my first substitute appearance following the injury. How fitting is it that my first minutes after the injury were against the same player and the same team that I had been injured against in the first place? Life works in mysterious ways at times.

But if you were to ask me what the biggest lesson I learned from what I went through is, I would say that the biggest thing I learned, which forms the basis for this book, is that every single one of us can learn something from other people's journeys, even people we seemingly have nothing in common with. I say that because after my injury I received thousands of letters, mainly from people in the United States and England. At first, all of the letters were from football fans, and these letters were usually notes of encouragement. However, when I actually returned to the pitch and started playing consistently again, the letters didn't stop. I kept receiving them, but their tone had changed. They were no longer coming from just football fans. I had people from all walks of life writing to me. As I read these new letters I began to read things like:

- Thank you for being an inspiration. I just lost my job, but seeing how positive you have been through your hardship has helped me to remain positive in mine.
- I also had an injury that left me unable to work and I just want to tell you that your story inspires me.
- Hello Steve, I am a teacher and I used your story in a class lesson today.
- Steve, this is Pastor so and so, I used your story in my sermon on forgiveness and perseverance today.

I learned right then and there that my story wasn't limited to sports and definitely not just to football. It was a story that others could learn from because it was a human story. It was a story that anyone could take encouragement from.

On the one hand, it was a story of loss, suffering, and hardship. But on the other, it was one of hope, perseverance, and overcoming. It was the realization that my story could reach people from all walks of life that initially led me to write this book. This book is not really an autobiography, although it contains many factual stories from my life and my career; it's more of a collection of thoughts on the experiences I went through and the lessons I learned from one of the most defining moments of my life.

I share plenty of stories from my childhood and teenage years because I want you to know how I ended up playing professionally in the first place, and how I ended up in Denver on that life-changing night; but the book is more about the challenges I faced after breaking my leg and how I was able to make a full recovery and return to the pitch. The journey back to the pitch was the hardest path I've ever had to walk. I had to accept that as hard as I worked in my physical therapy sessions, I may never make a full recovery and become the player that I could have been. I had to accept that I'd probably never really know how much of my career I truly lost. These were tough pills to swallow, and they still are. But, I was able to overcome all of my doubts and get back to playing.

Sure, I had dark days, but they never defeated me. I had a lot of doubts, but they never became my reality. When you're at the end of your rope, you have to believe that you'll get through what you are going through. It's always possible. That's the message I hope my story conveys.

This book began as a letter to myself more than anything. I wrote a lot in the days and months following the injury because I wanted to have an outlet for my frustrations and despair, but I also thought it would be good to record all of the small victories I gathered along the way to my ultimate goal of getting back out onto a football pitch. From the day of my injury until the next time I played a game as a starter, the exact time that elapsed was five hundred days. April 22, 2011, to September 2, 2012.

Five hundred days is a long time to wait for anything, but it feels even longer when the thing you're waiting for is the only thing you want. During the five hundred days between my injury and the first time I was named in the starting lineup for a game, I experienced the highest of highs and the lowest of lows.

Not many athletes can relate to having an entire stadium of forty thousand people, holding up a card with their jersey number while chanting their name for an entire minute. That was a very high moment. Another high was the first time I stepped back onto the field after my injury. This was the game I mentioned earlier, the one in which I switched jerseys after the game with the player who had injured me. We were playing Colorado again, and even though I wasn't fully fit for this game, my coach, Sigi Schmid, wanted to reward me for the work I had been putting in on the training pitch, and he also wanted me to get a taste of what was to come if I kept working hard to get back to full fitness.

Under normal circumstances I know he wouldn't have played me, because I wasn't quite ready yet, but he and I both knew that whenever my first appearance came there would be a big media circus around it, and so it was better for us to get that circus out of the way sooner rather than later. In the days leading up to that game I had been doing more drills with the rest of the team in practice. It was a big step forward for me to be in full-contact training, and I knew that I was very close to a complete recovery, but I wasn't quite there yet.

The previous week Sigi had named me in the game-day roster, but I never got into the game. I watched us tie Sporting Kansas 1-1. So even though he had put me on the game-day roster again for this particular game, it wasn't a guarantee that I was going to see any game time.

We were winning 2-0 with about twenty minutes to go and we had already made two subs. I was warming up behind one of the goals with Dave Tenney, the Sounders' fitness coach, and I kept looking over to our bench to try and get Sigi's attention so that he could put me in. He had only one more sub that he could make and I was praying that it would be me. But no matter how often I looked over at our bench to try and get his attention, we never made eye contact. I kept looking in his direction, but he never looked in mine even once. Time was slipping away.

And then something happened to diminish my chances of going in: Colorado scored! It was now 2-1 and there were only ten minutes left; I didn't think I would be going in. *Sigi will probably bring a defender on so he can tighten things up at the back,* I thought to myself. A few more minutes went by and he still wasn't looking in my direction. *He's never going to look over here.* I stopped warming up and just stood behind the goal watching the game.

With only five minutes left, I'd lost all hope of going to get into the game. I began looking ahead to the next game. But just as I was doing that Dave came up to me and told me that I was going in.

"Zakuani, are you ready?"

"Wait, what?" I replied as I tried to hide the look of confusion on my face.

"You're going in," Dave said with a smile.

I looked over to our bench and saw that all of our coaches were on their feet and they were motioning me over. A big smile came across my face as I jogged back toward our bench. The fans must have caught wind of what was going on because they began to applaud. The atmosphere inside CenturyLink Field was heating up; it was electric.

I took off my warm-up jersey and put on my game jersey for the first time in over a year. I'd missed the feeling of wearing a game jersey. I closed my eyes and soaked in the moment before I walked over to Sigi to get my final instructions.

"You're going in for Rosales. It's 2-1 and there's only five minutes left, so help us close out the game," Sigi told me as all of the assistant coaches wished me good luck.

"Okay."

"If you get a chance to run at their defense, do it. Otherwise, keep it simple."

"Okay," I replied as I started to feel butterflies in my stomach.

"You're going to go and play in your normal position on the left."

"Got it."

"And hey, enjoy it. You've worked for this."

He gave me a pat on the back and I walked over to the sideline to wait for my moment. The fans were up on their feet and singing my name. It was extremely loud. And then disaster struck, Colorado scored. 2-2. I couldn't believe it. *Sigi is going to change his mind and throw a defender in there so we don't lose this game,* I thought to myself. *He's going to call me back at any moment so he can put a defender in.* I better not look at him. I could feel Sigi looking over in my direction, but I refused to look over at him. Our roles were now reversed. He probably just wanted to give me an instruction to pass on to the team, but I wasn't taking any chances; I was not going to look at him.

I was extremely relieved to see that the Colorado goal was called back for offside. It was still 2-1. I was definitely going to go in. The ball went out of play and there was a break in the game. It was time to make the substitution. My name was announced over the PA system: "Entering the game, replacing Mauro Rosales, is number eleven, Steeeeeve Zakuuuaaaaniiiii!"

It was music to my ears. Seattle exploded! Cameras were flashing, people were cheering; it seriously felt like a mini-earthquake, and it was a surreal thing to experience. Even the players on the pitch were applauding for me. *This can't be my life*, I thought to myself as I jogged onto the field. I've heard the Sounders' fans make a lot of noise before—we all know how loud and passionate they are—but I had never heard them like this. Eddie Johnson, my friend and teammate at the time, said in an interview after the game that it was the loudest he had ever heard any stadium in his entire career. Sigi told soundersfc.com, "For sure the eruption of the crowd was as loud as I think I've ever heard it here. It was fantastic." That night, I was a worldwide trending topic on Twitter; this story had connected with people all over the globe.

But there were also some low moments during those five hundred days. My father always told me that in life you have to take the good with the bad, and that statement was a daily reality for me during those five hundred days. As high as the high moments were, they were few and far between. It was the low moments that were more of a daily, ongoing thing. Just like there aren't many athletes who have experienced the highs that I have and the outpouring of love that I received from the Sounders' fans in particular, there are even fewer who have been to the low valleys that I have been to or who have had to face the obstacles and fears that I did.

In those five hundred days I spent hundreds of hours having to silence the small voice in my head that was telling me all of the physical therapy and hard work that I was doing in the gym was pointless and wouldn't amount to anything. That small voice that felt it necessary to constantly remind me of everything that I had lost—my passion, my livelihood, my love—and everything that I was facing—uncertainty, doubt, identity crisis—was very difficult to ignore at times.

Up until this day people continue to tell me about their own struggles and how my story has given them the inspiration and strength to overcome. It was those conversations that led me to bring structure to all of the different writings and journal entries I had done during those five hundred days and to turn them into a story about hope and overcoming adverse circumstances.

One of my mentors, the bestselling author and inspirational speaker, Dr. Myles Munroe, told me that we should never give up during difficult times because there is always life after the storm. Well, I've been through the storm, and this book is proof that there is indeed life after the storm. It is, however, the lessons learned during the storm that define my journey. The things I faced that I never thought I would have to face as a professional athlete, those are the things that made my journey what it was.

My only hope with this book is that it will do one of three things:

- Give hope to anyone chasing a dream that they can achieve it no matter how big it is.
- Bring encouragement and inspiration to anyone who has gone, or is going, through a hardship and challenge of any kind.
- Share lessons learned in my own life, through the obstacles I have faced, that anyone facing an obstacle can relate to, identify with, and apply in their own lives so that they may also emerge better and stronger on the other side of their challenge.

I only had one goal after I suffered my injury and that goal was to play football again; even one more game would have been enough. I was able to do that and more. With this book I want to tell you how I did it. This is my story. I hope it can give you some inspiration as you go about life facing your own challenges.

Steve Zakuani
Portland, Oregon
June 2014

CHAPTER 2

THE BEAUTIFUL GAME

Soccer isn't the same as Bach or Buddhism. But it is often
more deeply felt than religion, and just as much a part
of the community's fabric, a repository of traditions.

—FRANKLIN FOER

For as long as I can remember I have always had a ball at my feet. At home I dribbled the ball around the furniture, through the hallway, and up and down the stairs. At school I couldn't wait until lunch break so that I could leave the classroom and go and play football in the park with my friends. On weekends I played for hours on the streets outside my house with the other neighborhood kids. The ball never left my side. It was all I knew and all I cared about.

The first time I knew that I wanted to play professional football for a living was in the summer of 1994 when we took a family vacation to a popular resort in England called Butlins. Apart from my immediate family, a bunch of my aunts, uncles, and cousins also made the trip to Butlins. And since it was summer time and school was out the resort was packed with lots of kids. The place was literally crawling with little kids, and there was about a ten to one ratio of kids to adults. Everywhere you turned there seemed to be a group of young kids, high off sugar, making loud noises and running around at full speed to nowhere in particular.

I was having the time of my life making friends with the other kids and we never seemed to run out of energy as we played around all day long. When we weren't sliding down the water slides, lying by the pool, or playing hide and seek in the amusement park, we were playing football in the massive grass area right by our hotel rooms. Sometimes it was fifteen on fifteen or twenty on twenty, there was never a referee, and there definitely wasn't much structure, but we played for hours on end without so much as a water break. The final score would usually be something like 19-17, 25-13, or 17-12.

But as much as I had fun playing football for several hours every day, that actually wasn't what made me fall in love with the game to the point that I wanted to make a living out of it. No, the thing that made me fall in love with football was what we did every evening after our three-hour game was finished. Without fail, every evening, after we were done playing, all of the kids would huddle around a television set and watch the World Cup.

The 1994 World Cup was being played in the United States and because of the time difference between the U.S. and Europe we often had to stay up really late to watch some of the games, but the lack of sleep was more than worth it. I remember being enamored of the Italian forward Roberto Baggio and his famous ponytail. The way he bamboozled the defenders with his skills left me mesmerized and made all of us want to be like him the next day when we played our own little game on that grass area. And then there was the Brazilian forward Romario. What a player! Speed, skill, agility, and the ability to score—he had it all. I wanted to be like these guys so bad. It was the '94 World Cup that planted the seed of wanting to play football for a living in me.

It wasn't just the spectacle I was seeing out on the pitch that drew me in; it was more than that. It was the emotions, the desire, the highs, the lows, and the passion that this sport evoked in people; that's what really hooked me in. Watching all of these different nations with different cultures embrace this one sport and play it with such passion and love left a huge impression on me. I had never seen anything unite so many different cultures from all over the world in the way that I was seeing football do. When a team was knocked out of the tournament, it wasn't just the fans in the stands who were crying; it was the players on the pitch, too, and some of them were crying even more than the fans were.

It was an incredible thing to witness, and as the tournament wore on and I watched more and more of it I began to see some of those same emotions I saw in the fans and the players on TV, begin to manifest in me. When the team that I wanted to win was defeated it would put me in a bad mood for the rest of the day. And if my team won I would run around the room celebrating as if I were the one who had scored the game-winning goal.

I can vividly remember the final of that World Cup. The game wasn't very memorable; it was 0-0 and had to be decided by penalty kicks. But it was the two best teams going head to head—Brazil versus Italy—and the two best players were going up against each other as well—Romario versus Baggio. As I fought off sleepiness I sat down on the floor with my eyes glued to our little television screen. I was sitting only about two feet away from the television because I wanted to get as close to the action and atmosphere as possible. A part of me was ecstatic to see the Brazilians lifting the trophy after beating the Italians 3-2 on penalties, but another part of me felt sick to my stomach to see Baggio with his head in his hands crying. Despite playing a phenomenal tournament and being one of the standout players he had missed a penalty in the shootout and was now inconsolable.

I had never seen anything bring out such an array of emotions in human beings the way that I saw football do. The Brazilian fans in the stands were jumping up and down in wild celebration; and the Italian fans were slumped down in their seats with tears in their eyes. How could a sport, a game, bring out so much passion and emotion in people? I was thousands of miles away from where the World Cup was taking place, but I could feel every emotion that those fans were feeling.

It was this power that I experienced from watching the World Cup that really caused me to fall in love with the beautiful game. During the 1994 World Cup I went from just liking football to passionately caring about it, and it was shortly after that World Cup final between Brazil and Italy that I decided I wanted to become like Baggio and Romario when I grew up. Whenever someone asked me what I wanted to do when I was older, my reply was automatic: "I'm going to play professional football." I always had my response ready. The 1994 World Cup had changed the way I looked at football, and after I returned home from that Butlins vacation the ball never left my side.

As I look back on my life it seems as though change and adversity are the only constants. I was born in the Democratic Republic of Congo in 1988. The country was known as Zaire at the time, and like those in many African nations we had faced war and political unrest in the Congo. I have vivid memories of seeing rebel soldiers patrolling the streets with heavy artillery, and I even remember a time when some soldiers, armed with guns, violently forced their way into our family home. I don't remember why they came, I just remember that they did, and I'm sure we weren't the only African family during that time to experience such an incident.

Due to the instability and unrest in the Congo, many families migrated to Europe in those days, and my family was no exception. We left the Congo and moved to London, England, when I was four years old. This was the first big change I had ever faced in my life but it certainly wouldn't be the last. Moving from the warm African continent to a cold and rainy England at age four when you don't speak the language and don't know anything about the culture is about as big a change as you can get. I had a very hard time at first in London as I tried to adapt to my new surroundings.

One of the hardest things to deal with in life is change. Change brings the unexpected and the unknown. It's much easier to go through life if you know what to expect and when to expect it than to have to deal with sudden changes that can disrupt even the best-laid plans. Change often arrives unannounced and when we least expect it. Naturally, humans are creatures of comfort and we are all resistant to change because it destroys our comfort zones. But there is simply no escaping change, it happens to everything and everyone.

Change, along with death and taxes, is the only guarantee in life and the sooner we can accept that nothing stays the same the more equipped we will be to deal with the changes as they come. Nothing stays the same. Ever. Life is about growing and evolving. It's about change.

From the very moment I felt that tackle hit my leg I knew that my life had changed forever. I also knew that I could either let it break me or I could use it to help me grow and become stronger. I chose the second option and began spending my spare time in the hospital, and later at home when I was discharged, reading up on people throughout history who have faced hardships and overcome them.

I wanted to learn some secrets and strategies that would help me to overcome adversity just as they had, sometimes against even more difficult odds than the ones I was facing. As I read biographies, stories, and articles, and watched documentaries, I started to see that most great people throughout history are actually known for the things that they overcame and fought against. Martin Luther King, Jr., is known for overcoming racial prejudice and setting in motion the changes that led to African Americans receiving their civil rights. Mahatma Gandhi is remembered for standing up for himself and his fellow Indians against the British Empire as he demanded independence from their colonial rule. Nelson Mandela is etched in history because he gave up his freedom for twenty-seven years so that equality would be the norm in South Africa.

Those three, along with Mother Teresa and Abraham Lincoln, were just some of the people whose stories I read and studied in depth in the months after my injury, and I saw that they would always be remembered for the adversities they had overcome. Their willingness to confront the changes and obstacles they faced has inspired millions and will continue to do so for generations to come.

Reading their stories gave me added motivation and encouragement to stand tall in the face of my own adversity. "No one is ever remembered for the adversity they avoided or the hardships they ran from," I wrote down on a piece of paper as I lay on my hospital bed. "We remember those who looked defeat in the eye and emerged victorious." It was in that moment that I decided to embrace the change that had taken place in my life because of my injury and to use it as a springboard to a bigger and better future. I didn't want to be remembered as someone who caved in under pressure; I wanted to be known as someone who not only embraced but also overcame his adversity.

I've been on well over one hundred flights in my life but I still remember the very first one like it was yesterday. I remember standing at the gate looking at the plane that was to take us from Congo to Europe and being amazed at how big it was. I didn't understand how this thing was going to leave the ground. I'd never seen such a big machine before. This big metal tube was our escape from the unrest in the Congo and our key to what we hoped would be a better life in England.

I really didn't have much of an attachment to the Congo because I was only four years old when we moved, but I was still old enough to know that I would miss my grandparents, cousins, and friends that we were leaving behind. I don't remember much about the flight itself, but I can recall feeling slightly anxious at the fact that we were leaving behind everything I had ever known to go to an unknown place and start a new life. I was only four but I was aware of what was happening.

Before we got to London we had a layover in Brussels, Belgium. As we walked through the airport I kept staring at all of those strangers. I had never been around white people before and I couldn't help but stare at them trying to figure out why they looked so much different than I did. They seemed to be everywhere. I couldn't stare for too long, though, because we were only in Belgium for a short time before we had to make our way to the gate where we would catch the flight that would take us to our new home and our new life in London.

From the moment we arrived in London I began to face adversity. My siblings and I were the outcasts at school because we weren't able to communicate with the other students. We knew how to speak French and we also understood some local Congolese dialects but we had never been around English speakers before. That was just one of the many things that made us stand out. This was a new and frightening experience for my siblings and me.

I have three sisters, Angela, Admira, and Claudia, and two brothers, Gabriel and Sosthene. At the time, only Angela, Gabriel, and me were old enough to attend school and so we hung out together while all the other kids stayed away from us. People are usually drawn to each other because of the things they have in common. On all of the teams I have been on, if there are three or four players who speak the same language they will normally spend a lot of time together during team activities, and it's not that they don't like their other teammates; it's simply a case of being able to relate much easier to those who share the same language and culture as them.

When I was sixteen I spent a week in Spain training with the Spanish team Real Valladolid. I didn't speak Spanish at the time and I felt isolated from all of the other players. After about three or four days one of the players, Alex, said something to me in English as we sat around in the locker room. For the rest of my time there I tried to spend more time with Alex than with anyone else simply because I had something more in common with him than with anyone else on that team.

This happens in all walks of life and in every workplace. Think about the people you are really good friends with and then ask yourself why you are friends with these people. It's probably because you share the same hobbies, culture, interests, views, career, or have something else in common that unites you and makes you easily relate to one another. When you have nothing in common with people it's very hard to build any kind of friendship with them, and that's why I had no friends when I first went to school in London. I had absolutely nothing in common with any of the kids in my class. I was the new kid, the outsider. Their bonds had already been formed and there was no way I was going to gain their acceptance just like that.

In those early days, when I didn't have any friends, I stayed extra close to my siblings. The other kids made no attempts to reach out to us, so we kind of just stayed in the background. We were in a new country, living a new life, around a new language, and we had no friends. I was four years old.

Things stayed that way for quite a while until one day I was asked to play football with the other kids during playtime, known as recess to my American friends. I don't remember why they had never asked me to play before or why they thought to ask me to play on this particular day but I gladly accepted their offer and joined them. Maybe they were low on numbers, or maybe they felt sorry for me; I didn't know and I didn't care. I was just happy to be included in an activity with all of the other kids for once. I loved my siblings but I was getting enough of them at home, so it was getting quite boring to have to play with them at school as well.

Even though this particular day would be the first time that I had really kicked a football, I was already quite familiar with the sport because my dad watched a lot of it at home. Back in the early to mid-nineties the Italian league was the best in the world and we would watch it at home every Sunday without fail. Italy had all of the best teams and players. AC Milan, Inter, Juventus, Sampdoria, Napoli, Roma, Lazio, and Parma were just some of the teams I was already familiar with. I also knew a lot of the best players like Diego Maradona, Alessandro Del Piero, Paolo Maldini, Ruud Gullit, Marco Van Basten, and Fabrizio Ravanelli.

In those days the Italian league had the same appeal that the English league has today. The games usually came on TV every Sunday and it became a weekly ritual for my older brother, Gabriel, and I, to join my dad in the living room so we could watch the game of the week. After the game we would sometimes run back to our room and roll a bunch of socks up into a big round, sometimes oblong ball, and play against each other. I had never really played football outside of the house before the day that the other kids asked me to join them because before then all of my playing had taken place in the bedroom with a ball-sock against my brother.

I feel very blessed to have had firsthand experience of the power football has to unite people all over the world. I've traveled to several countries and interacted with different cultures and even if I didn't speak their language once a football ball was thrown into the mix we all became friends and had a good time. This invitation that the other kids extended to me so I could play with them was the first time I would experience the unifying power of football, because as soon as the other kids saw what I could do with a ball everything changed.

The months of no interaction, of not being included, and of being the outsider were gone just like that; they all fell in love with me. It's not like I had given them money, toys, or cookies. All I had done was dribble the ball around all of them. I hadn't tried to gain their acceptance, it just happened.

Soon after that day I became known as the star footballer amongst all my classmates. My lifelong bond with this sport was born on that school playground back in 1993. I had a new identity. I was no longer the weird African kid who couldn't speak English; I was now the best footballer in the class. I liked this new identity because it made everyone embrace me and I became quite popular. Even though I was still struggling to master the English language I was now looking forward to that daily twenty-minute break between classes when I could get outside and play football with everyone else. I had no idea that I had just discovered the passion I would end up devoting my life to for the next two decades.

In those days I played football because it made me friends and gave me an identity. Being known as the best player in my class made me feel important and popular. I was never the kid who was picked last when we were selecting teams, and so in many ways my self-esteem and sense of self-worth were derived from my ability to play football well.

Professional athletes, whether they are aware of it or not, tend to view who they are as people and what they do for a living as the same thing. I am a footballer. I am a runner. I am a basketball player. We become what we do. We are synonymous with our sport. We are introduced to people with, "This is the footballer I was telling you about" or "This is Steve from the (insert team name)." We get so used to it. Our identity is intertwined with our sport. Most of the time, there's nothing wrong with this, but after my injury I would learn that there is a big danger in getting your identity as a person from what you do for a living because playing a sport, or having any career, is only temporary but your identity should be forever. What you do and who you are should be different because you can stop playing a sport, or stop having the job that you have, but you can never stop being you. You should always have an identity outside of your profession, no matter what your profession is.

It's a major shock to your system to have to find a new identity when you change jobs or retire from your sport if you've always equated who you are with what you do. Imagine doing something for twenty years and it's all you have ever known or cared about. It's a part of you; it's who you are. And then one day you retire because your body can no longer do it. The next morning when you wake up, you'll quickly realize that although you've retired from your sport you haven't retired from being yourself. You haven't stopped being you. And so it's important that you have a preexisting identity outside of what you do because if you don't you will have to spend your time after retirement trying to figure out who you really are; and that can be a painful process. You will have to figure out where to get your self-worth and self-esteem now that the thing that gave it to you is no longer a part of your life. These were issues I would have to deal with later in my life. For the time being, however, I was just happy to be known as the star footballer at school.

There were other adversities we had to deal with as a family when we first moved to Europe from Africa. When we arrived we lived with some relatives in East London because we didn't have a place of our own. Their house wasn't very big to begin with, and trying to fit two different families under one roof made it even smaller. After a few months we finally got our own little space in a place called Stonebridge.

Stonebridge is well known for being a low-income area filled with gangs and violence. It's located in the Northwest area of London. We were in Stonebridge for about a year or so before we settled into a house in a place called Tottenham, which is in North London. We would remain in Tottenham for several years. Just like Stonebridge, Tottenham was also a very low-income, crime-ridden area of London, and it was filled with many immigrant and refugee families from the Congo, Ghana, Nigeria, Somalia, Turkey, Jamaica, Uganda, and many more countries. So even though we had left Africa, at times it seemed as though we were still there because almost everyone around us had come from there too. Most of my friends growing up were from the Congo, or from another African country. I had some Jamaican and Caribbean friends as well as white English friends, but the majority of my friends were from somewhere in Africa.

Although I was now living in England, my home life was still very African. The food we ate, the music that we listened to, and the way we spoke to one another at home was the same as it had been when we were back in the Congo. In those days, a lot of the white English kids in my class were having their first contact with black African kids and they made fun of everything about us from our last names to our accents.

People, kids especially, tend to poke fun at things they don't understand or aren't familiar with, and since the kids in my class were completely unfamiliar with me they poked fun at me a lot. Now, I'm not saying that every single one of my classmates was a white English kid and that I was the only foreigner, not at all. There were other black kids in the class, as well as some Turkish, Somali, and Asian ones, but many of them had been born in England, and were fluent in English, which allowed them to fit in better with the English kids. I wasn't born in England, I couldn't speak English very well, and I also stood out by the way I dressed.

I was sometimes embarrassed to speak French with my parents if I knew that an English kid or family were within earshot of our conversation. When my classmates would ask me where I was from I would sometimes say I was from France or Belgium and they would believe me because French was my first language. Being from Africa meant that you were seen as different, poor, and weird, which is why I claimed to be from a European country. Needless to say, as a young kid I was extremely embarrassed to be from Africa because of all the things my classmates, who knew no better, thought about African people. It was much easier to lie and say that I was French than to stand up for myself and try to defend a continent that is home to over a billion people.

In my young mind, the equation was very simple: Africa equaled weird and different, whereas Europe equaled cool and normal. Looking back now it feels ridiculous that I wanted to be from anywhere other than Africa because as I've grown older and matured I've become extremely proud of the fact that I was born in the Congo. I even have a tattoo of Africa on my left shoulder. I'm very proud to be from the Congo and I wanted to permanently remind myself of where I come from, hence the tattoo. But back then, when I was only five or six years old, I was just trying to make friends and fit in. I tried to minimize the extent to which I stood out by disowning my heritage.

I think one of the great things about being a child is that you are so innocent and unaware of some of the things that adults are aware of. It's only when I write of these experiences now that I realize how crazy it was for a six-year-old kid to be made fun of for his name, accent, and other trivial things over which he has no control, because I don't remember during that time, when I lived it, spending too much time being hurt by my treatment. I never cried or complained and I was oblivious to how insensitive it was for my classmates to make fun of me. My only desire was to do everything that I could to make friends and have people like me.

The most powerful tool, which at the time was the only tool I had to make friends, was a football. As soon as I was outside playing with the other kids, our ethnicities, backgrounds, names, and accents meant nothing. We were united by this game, which was our common love. It still amazes me when I think about how powerful a tool football has been in my life. It is the tool that has united me with people of all backgrounds and cultures, has taken me all over the globe, and has brought me into experiences that still give me goose bumps when I think back on them.

One of my first goose-bump-worthy experiences happened when I signed onto one of the best youth football teams in the world when I was only nine years old. It was the summer of 1997 when I got word that some scouts from Arsenal Football Club had seen me play and wanted to sign me. At the time I didn't like Arsenal very much. I was actually a huge fan of one of their big rivals, Manchester United, primarily because of their French player, the great Eric Cantona. I loved this man. I loved everything about him, from the way he wore his collar up, to the way he celebrated his goals. If I saw him score on a Sunday I would be on the school playground mimicking his celebration on Monday morning.

Another reason why I didn't really like Arsenal was because I lived in Tottenham. Tottenham's team, Tottenham Hotspurs FC, is and always will be Arsenal's biggest rival. The two teams have a long history of bad blood and because I was living in Tottenham I liked them a bit more than Arsenal. With that in mind, I guess it's quite understandable when I say that I wasn't immediately excited about this Arsenal opportunity. If it had been Manchester United that had

wanted to sign me at that time I would have gone crazy with excitement, but it was Arsenal, a team that I didn't like or care for very much.

Over time, however, that lack of enthusiasm I had for Arsenal
would give way to pure joy and exhilaration after I had my first training
session with them a few days after finding out they were interested in
me. From then on Arsenal became my favorite team. I spent five years
playing for them, and they taught me everything I know about playing
the beautiful game of football.

Shortly after I began playing football at school my dad took my
older brother and me to join club teams. My brother played for a team
called Dagenham United, and I played for a team called Barking Colts.
Both teams were amateur clubs and were based in East London. In
England Sunday League Football, as we call it, is huge. All over the
country kids as young as seven or eight, and adults as old as forty or
fifty, play on amateur club teams that play their games on Sundays.
Every club has several age groups, and playing Sunday League Football
is the easiest way for professional teams to discover players because
they are always sending scouts to watch the games. In fact, it was while
I was playing on a Sunday League team that I was scouted by Arsenal.

I loved my time with Barking Colts because it was the first time I
got to play football in an organized fashion. My experience before then
had been limited to a school playground or the street in front of my
house, where I played with my friends with no rules, no goalies (no kid
ever wanted to go in goal), and no referees. With Barking Colts, I got
to play with referees, linesmen, goalies, and proper rules.

The only thing I didn't like about playing for Barking Colts was
that we would always lose 7-0 to a team called Redbridge United. I'm
being dead serious. Every single time we played them they would beat
us 7-0. It was never 7-1, 8-0, or 9-0; it was always 7-0. It must have
happened four or five times. After a couple of years of suffering that
embarrassment I did what any kid in my position would do. I left
Barking Colts and went to play for Redbridge United. I felt kind of bad
leaving the friends I'd made at Barking Colts, but even at my young
age I knew that playing with the better players at Redbridge United
would be better for my development as a player. And after all, "If you
can't beat them, join them."

At Redbridge United, playing with better players than the ones
I had played with at Barking Colts, my game improved considerably.
I no longer had to try and dribble past three or four players just to

get a shot on goal. I was now playing alongside the best kids at my age that weren't already signed to a professional youth team. David Beckham, Ashley Cole, Jermaine Defoe, Teddy Sheringham, and Rio Ferdinand are just some of the famous English players who also began their careers by playing Sunday League Football in London. In fact, David Beckham had played for a team called Ridgeway Rovers and they happened to be in the same league, The Echo League, as my team, Redbridge United. He had played in that league several years before I ever came along, but whenever we went to play against Ridgeway Rovers we would see photos of him all over their clubhouse.

We played against Ridgeway several times while I was at Redbridge and each time, without fail, our coach would tell us that we needed to win because this was the team that David Beckham had played on. Whenever he said that I thought to myself, "Well, it's not like he's playing on the team now, so why does that matter?"

It was in the summer of 1997, while I was playing in a tournament for Redbridge United somewhere in East London, that a scout from Arsenal saw me play and invited me to come and train with the team. As I've already mentioned, most kids would have been excited about that invitation because Arsenal were a great team with one of the best youth teams in England, but I really wasn't that excited about it at first.

I was feeling somewhat indifferent as my dad drove me to the stadium, which was only about a twelve-minute drive from our house, for my first training session with them. That indifferent feeling evaporated as soon as I shook Liam Brady's hand. Liam Brady was the director of the Arsenal youth academy. Years earlier he had been a great player for Arsenal, the Italian team Juventus, and for his country, Ireland. It was very special to be able to meet him in person and to shake his hand at such a young age; Liam Brady was a living legend.

Once he had given my dad and me a tour of the stadium and sat us down in his office I knew that Arsenal was where I wanted to be. He gave us an overview of what Arsenal stood for and of their commitment to developing young players. I heard all about the history of the club, their greatest players ever, and about their new French coach, who had just arrived from Japan. His name was Arsene Wenger.

Arsene wasn't very well known in England when he first arrived to coach Arsenal, and most people openly criticized his appointment. In the years to come, however, he would prove to be one of the most successful coaches to ever coach in England, as he completely revolutionized Arsenal. He turned them from being just another good team to being arguably the very best team. The fans loved him because he brought players such as Thierry Henry, Robert Pires, Freddie Ljungberg, Robin Van Persie, and Patrick Vieira to Arsenal, and they all brought the club a lot of success.

After Liam Brady told me all about this great club I knew that Arsenal was where I wanted to be. The next night I had my first practice with the team. That practice led to a five-year stay at the club as I went on to play over one hundred fifty games for the Arsenal youth academy. I had some pretty incredible experiences as I traveled to play in tournaments and showcases all over the world, while representing the red and white colors of Arsenal.

Just five years after arriving in England I had signed onto one of the best youth teams in the world. My dream of doing what I had seen Baggio and Romario do was beginning to take shape. The weird African kid turned school football star was about to begin a journey that would introduce him to lifelong friends; bring him pain and joy, success and failure, fear and faith; while teaching him deep, amazing, and meaningful things about himself, others, and life. It was a journey that would take him from London to Akron to Seattle and to Portland, with pit stops all over the globe along the way.

CHAPTER 3
TOTTENHAM

The world is a book and those who do
not travel read only one page.

—AUGUSTINE OF HIPPO

Tottenham is a rough place. Those of us who have lived there have always known this, but in the summer of 2011 the whole world caught a glimpse of just how turbulent and volatile a place Tottenham can be.

Tottenham was the birthplace of what came to be known as the London Riots. These riots, in which stores were vandalized, buildings were burned to the ground, police cars were overturned, businesses were broken into, and homes were destroyed, were sparked by the death of Mark Duggan, who was a black Tottenham resident who died at the hands of local police. At first the riots were only taking place in London, but eventually they spread to other cities until there was looting, violence, vandalism, and tension all over England. This led the London Riots to become known as the England Riots. For about a week there was nonstop rioting on the streets of several cities across England, from morning to evening people all over the country destroyed the very communities that they lived in; and to think that it all began in my home city, Tottenham.

The riots were initially sparked by the angry response of the local community to the death of Mark Duggan by a policeman. Tottenham's black community blamed racial prejudice for the killing, but the circumstances that led to the shooting are still heavily debated three years on. Initially the police report stated that Mark Duggan fired the first shot at police as he exited a taxi. The cop who shot and killed him did so only in self-defense. That was the police's official version of events, but from the moment the police report made its way on to the evening news people in Tottenham were suspicious about that particular version of events because several eyewitnesses reported that Mark Duggan had been unarmed.

As a result, a large group of Tottenham residents, both black and white, marched to the local police station demanding to know why an unarmed man had been shot and killed. As the group closed in on the police station an altercation between a cop and one of the marchers sparked the burning of a police car, which proved to be the first violent act in what would become the England Riots. Things got worse when it was revealed that the police report had been false and that Mark Duggan had indeed been unarmed. Once that information was made public full scale rioting began taking place all over England.

Tottenham wasn't the prettiest of places to begin with, but after the riots the place looked like a scene from the Apocalypse. Buildings that once stood one hundred feet tall had been reduced to ashes. Cars had been burned and overturned. Glass from smashed apartment windows decorated the concrete pavements. Some local family-owned businesses that took years to build and had been in the community for as long as I can remember were destroyed in seconds. Can you imagine watching your lifelong work being burned to the ground right before your eyes? It was an astonishing time in Tottenham.

The irony of the situation is that even though the people behind these riots were initially angry with the police they actually ended up trashing and destroying their own neighborhood as they ruined things that their parents and grandparents had spent years building.

As I watched the riots in my hometown unfold from across the Atlantic I couldn't say I was surprised that such a thing could happen in Tottenham. I wasn't sitting there in disbelief at what I was seeing, because having grown up there I knew that Tottenham was a pressure cooker that was ready to explode at any time. I had seen firsthand the poverty and daily grind that many families encountered in their lives. There was always tension just beneath the surface of everyday life in Tottenham.

Growing up I saw some of my friends go in and out of prison for crimes like burglary, drug selling, and domestic violence. Some people I knew passed away before their time as they were murdered by former friends or rival gangs. It was a cutthroat environment to live in even on the best of days. I guess my point is that when you live in a place like that the world becomes a very small place. All you know is what you see and experience on a daily basis.

This is probably why so many gifted individuals that I knew growing up never really accomplished much in life. They never became all that they could have been because their worldview and aspirations were limited to, and stifled by, their surroundings. They knew of no other life and they had no idea that there was a world beyond Tottenham. They had no idea that there was a world beyond the constant sound of police sirens, violent gang altercations, and rampant drug use.

Tottenham was a massive melting pot of everything you would not want in a society. It had a way of draining people's dreams and ambitions. It limited what you expected from life and taught you that you probably wouldn't ever make it out of there and become something worth becoming. If you lived in Tottenham, then Tottenham was your whole world.

The crime and drugs became normal over the years. It was almost weird if you went a couple of days without seeing weed or crack. I don't have the exact statistic but I do know that teenage pregnancy was very high because I saw teenaged mothers every day on my way home from school. I love Tottenham and I am happy to have grown up there because I had to grow up very fast and I learned things there that I may not have learned elsewhere, but it had a way of hampering your ability to dream big. If someone found out that you were from Tottenham they almost expected you to become a failure in life because people from Tottenham generally didn't amount to much.

There were even teachers at my school who believed that I wouldn't achieve much in life; they were certain I would fail because I was from Tottenham. A teacher should never say anything like that to a student, but at the time I just accepted what they told me and believed it.

We had no worthy role models in Tottenham. The people I looked up to and wanted to be like sold drugs, had multiple women, and wore expensive jewelry that they paid for with illegal money. In recent years this reality of Tottenham has slowly begun to change as individuals from there have achieved success in sports and entertainment. Adele is from Tottenham. She's the most famous Tottenham-related success story, but there are others. Wretch 32 and Chip are two rappers from Tottenham who have had number one hit records and are now known all over England. There are some professional footballers playing in various leagues all over the world who have also emerged from Tottenham and are enjoying really strong, successful careers.

These kinds of role models never existed when I was growing up. We didn't have anyone to look up to who we could recognize as our own. Every successful person we saw on television didn't look, talk, or dress like we did, and they weren't from where we were from. I am happy to see that this is changing and it gives me great hope that the next generation of kids from Tottenham will take success to an even higher level as they begin to break the stereotypes that my generation began to put cracks in.

As a young kid, however, I never imagined a life beyond Tottenham, because the things I saw every day made it impossible to think of anything other than my immediate surroundings. It was in this area that football became my saving grace and taught me how to dream of a bigger and better life beyond Tottenham.

Playing for the Arsenal youth academy allowed me to travel all over Europe before I even hit puberty. As a young boy I was playing in football tournaments in countries as far away and exotic as Andorra. I traveled to Belgium multiple times and also to Italy. I played tournaments in the Netherlands and all over England. Every few months I would be on a plane to a different location far, far away from Tottenham.

I began to encounter diverse cultures and ethnicities. I got to see a world without crime, drugs, and teenage pregnancies. I got to play against the best youth teams in the world, teams such as Ajax, Lazio, Anderlecht, Liverpool, Chelsea, Atletico Madrid, and more. Teams like Barcelona, Real Madrid, and Manchester United also entered some of the same tournaments my Arsenal team was a part of. I can't emphasize enough how life-changing all of these experiences were. Whereas most of the kids I grew up with never left our street, I was able to leave not only our street but also our city and our country as I went and saw the world.

By the age of thirteen I had travelled more than many adults ever will. I have vivid memories of some of these trips even fifteen years on because they were so impactful. I remember when we flew to Andorra to compete in a tournament against some other elite youth football teams from around the world. As our plane descended on this beautiful country I caught a glimpse of the clear waters, the sun was shining, and there was so much greenery. I remember thinking to myself that this was the most beautiful thing I had ever seen in my life. The contrast between the gray and gloomy Tottenham skies and what I was now witnessing was night and day.

Our hotel was phenomenal. Everything from the pools and hot tubs to the breakfast buffets and tasty dinners was first class. Maybe some of my teammates were used to this kind of living, but I certainly wasn't. Back at home I shared a room and sometimes a bed with one of my siblings. We shared clothes, and there were days when we shared the bathtub in the mornings before school so we could utilize the limited hot water that was available to us. These aren't bad memories, quite the opposite in fact, because it was those things that taught me to be grateful for any and everything that I may have in the future. I learned to be content and to appreciate a lot of things that others may take for granted because growing up I had to make the most of what I was given. I had two wonderful parents, who always did their best and made sure that we had what we needed. I still don't know how my mother fed seven or eight mouths every night or how my father was able to provide for all of our needs regardless of what they were.

My home life was simple and I loved it, but seeing the things I saw on this Andorra trip definitely opened my eyes to some of the finer things in life. When I think back on that trip I tend to think about the hotel, the food, the hot tubs, and the weather. I hardly ever think about the actual football part of the trip. I would love to say that the reason for this is because I was just so overwhelmed by the beauty of my surroundings that football just kind of faded into the background, but the truth is that we didn't have a very good tournament. I've tried to forget about the football on that trip ever since I first got home from it because it was a painful experience.

For some reason we struggled in almost every game and we were eventually knocked out of the tournament when we lost 6-1 to the Spanish team Atletico Madrid. It still hurts to think about that one even fourteen years on. They outplayed us in every area of the pitch and were worthy winners on the day. It was the worst defeat I ever suffered in the five years I spent playing for the Arsenal youth team.

But in spite of what happened on the pitch I will always remember that trip as being the one that really showed me that there was a world outside of Tottenham, that there was so much more to this world than what I had been exposed to up until that point. Football was giving me some amazing life experiences and I began to realize that being a footballer would be a great way to see the world, stay in nice hotels, and play the sport I loved for a living. I was getting a taste of traveling while pursuing and engaging my passion, and I didn't want it to ever stop. This is what life is about, I would think to myself. And I made a decision to give everything I had to making my dream come true. Being able to travel and see the world instilled in me a desire to make something of my life. I didn't want to die in Tottenham like so many of my friends had done.

Whenever I came back to Tottenham after one of my trips dressed in Arsenal gear from head to toe I would be the center of attention. The other kids at school and in my neighborhood would want to hear about my travels, my experiences, and whether we had won or not. As I began to recount my tales they would be captivated and mesmerized by my vivid descriptions of the foods we ate, the hotels we stayed in, and the planes we flew on. I would tell them everything there was to know about Italian people and Spanish people. I would tell them what it feels like to look down at the earth from the window of a 747. I would talk about a world that was so far removed from our everyday surroundings, a world that they could only see with their imagination. Even back then I understood how privileged I was to be able to do what I was doing.

Three times a week I would leave my friends in Tottenham to go and train with Arsenal. It was always a welcome escape. After being at school all day surrounded by all the negative things you'd want your children to avoid it was a blessing to be able to go and train with Arsenal in the evenings and feed my passion.

Football became my escape from everything. And I'm thankful because a lot of my childhood friends didn't have that kind of escape. They never got the opportunities to leave our neighborhood and see the world like I did. Maybe this is a small reason why many of them fell into drugs and crime but I didn't. It's hard to sell drugs if you are in Italy playing against the best Italian youth teams one month and then in Belgium a couple of months later playing in another tournament. Simply put, football saved me from a life of drugs and crime.

Arsenal used to give us free tickets to every home game. My dad and I went to as many games as we could because we both loved to watch the likes of Thierry Henry, Robert Pires, Freddie Ljungberg, and Dennis

Bergkamp scoring goals and playing beautiful football. I would always sit in the North Bank. Each stand in the stadium had a name (the Clock End, the East Stand, the West Stand, and the North Bank). Our tickets were always in the North Bank, which was right behind one of the goals.

I can still remember the feelings of exhilaration that would run through my veins as I jumped up and down with thirty-eight thousand other Gooners (the official name for an Arsenal fan is a "Gooner" from Arsenal's nickname, the Gunners) as we celebrated yet another Thierry Henry goal. With every game that I attended I fell more in love with the club until Arsenal was in my blood. They were my team. Eric Cantona and Manchester United were a thing of the past because it was all about Arsenal now. I no longer just wanted to be a professional footballer; I now wanted to be a professional footballer for Arsenal. It had to be them and only them.

At the time I didn't realize that only an extremely small percentage of players ever make it through all the age groups in the youth team and all the way up to the first team. I just assumed that because I was doing well in the youth team I would automatically progress through the ranks until I was running out on the pitch alongside my favorite players.

My heart was so set on this dream that on the day Arsenal called my house at the end of the 2001-2002 season to let me know that they would not be renewing my contract for the next season I felt as though a part of my heart had been pierced with the sharpest of knives. It was the worst possible news. One minute I was known in the neighborhood as the kid who played for Arsenal, and the next I was back to being normal.

There was nothing special about me anymore because what had always made me different was that I was living a life that no other kid around me was living. No one travelled like I did. They didn't know anything about other cultures like I did; all they knew was Tottenham and the struggles that existed there. And now I was right back there with them.

My identity had been taken from me. I didn't know who I was in that moment. My dream had been stripped from me and I was back to square one. It wasn't until Arsenal released me that I realized just how much of my life had been invested into that dream. I had given five years of my life to that club and I had met some of my best friends there. When they told me that I was being released and wouldn't be offered a new contract it crushed me. I couldn't believe it. I felt so lost because that was all I had known. I would no longer be able to walk into class with my Arsenal jacket as I bragged about my latest trip or my latest goal.

It was the first time that the lesson that we should never equate who we are with what we do was taught to me. Who we are should always be separate from what we do because when we wrap our identity in what we do, we risk losing ourselves when what we do is taken from us. I also learned that when you begin to dream big you open up the possibility of failing big as well. They go hand in hand.

An easy way to measure a person's maturity is to see how they manage or respond to negative changes. When something bad happens to them, are they calm, rational, and ready to bounce back? Or do they panic, lose all rationale, and think that their life is over? Mature people are those who are able to take the blows that life deals them in their stride while keeping a clear perspective on the bigger picture. Immature people do the opposite. They focus only on the event that has occurred, they lose a sense of the bigger picture and end up making rash, emotional, in-the-moment decisions that they wouldn't normally make. With that definition of maturity in mind, I see that when I encountered the negative change of Arsenal releasing me at age fourteen I was very immature about it. I didn't respond well at all.

I think I had a right to be upset at some level, and maybe even angry. I had given so much of my time, effort, energy, and dedication to that dream, so to have it end just like that was a tough pill to swallow. However, the way I responded was not very good at all. It's true that I was young and that most teenagers wouldn't have responded well either, but I think I went a bit overboard in that I began to live a life that was completely opposite to the one I had been living before.

My hunger and passion for football dwindled significantly once the Arsenal chapter was done and I was no longer flying to exotic destinations and getting to watch Thierry Henry every week. Now that I was back to being just like all the other neighborhood kids I began to behave like them too. Gone were the flights, the hotels, and the tales of my adventures across the big beautiful world that existed outside of Tottenham. I was no longer special or different and I found that the distractions that come with being a teenager who lives in a low-income area like Tottenham, distractions that I had once been able to easily avoid, suddenly seemed irresistible, and I gave into them.

There were now times where I would spend all day with my friends who were selling and taking drugs. I never actually did any drugs, but even just being around that environment exposed me to some really dark things. I saw firsthand what heavy drug use and alcohol abuse can do to people. There were gang fights as well as a lot of unprotected sex that led to a lot of teenage pregnancies. Many low-income or ghetto areas all over the world contain these very same things, so I'm not saying that the things I saw were unique to Tottenham. There are some people reading this book who will know exactly what I am talking about because they also lived through similar experiences in their mid- to late teens. I've met people from all four corners of the globe who can share similar stories to mine; some of theirs are worse than mine, and others are not as bad. But the experiences are pretty much the same.

It's only when I look back on my teenage years that I realize how crazy it was to be exposed to some of the things that I was on a daily basis, because at the time it felt like I was just hanging out with my friends, friends who just happened to sell and take drugs. When Arsenal left my life I was drawn to the appeal of the lifestyle my friends were living, so even though I had two parents who taught me right from wrong and instilled morals and values in me it wasn't enough to protect me from the extremely attractive temptations that existed all around me. Some of the things I did in the months following my release from Arsenal included sneaking out of the house to attend parties and skipping class to hang out with girls.

There was one day where I got dressed in my school uniform, said goodbye to my parents, and left the house as if I were going to school. But instead of taking the bus that normally took me to school, I took a different bus. I was on my way to a friend's house. We had decided to skip school that day because we wanted to go into the city and enjoy ourselves. At his house I changed out of my uniform and put on some regular clothes—jeans, a t-shirt, and a hoodie. We ordered some Chinese food and listened to rap music. At the time my favorite rapper was Biggie, and I used to play his Ready to Die album on repeat several days at a time.

This wasn't the first time I had skipped school, but it was the first time I was planning to skip an entire day of school. In the past there had been times where I had shown up for about half the day before I went missing for the other half.

At about eleven in the morning, when I was supposed to be in geography class, we turned Biggie off, finished off our special fried rice, and headed for the city. We took the tube to Leicester Square and headed straight for HMV. HMV was one of the largest music stores in England and, being the lover of music that I am, I enjoyed going to this store because you could go in and listen to all of the latest records from around the world without having to spend any money. To my younger readers, this probably doesn't sound that exciting because they've grown up in the YouTube era when you can go and find any song in the world without having to leave your bed, but trust me: back then HMV was the place to be.

After HMV we walked into a bunch of different clothing stores and arcades in Leicester Square, Piccadilly Circus, and Oxford Street. When we weren't in a store or at the arcade we were on the street trying to talk to every single girl we saw, even though any girl we came across that day had to be older than us, since all of the girls who were our age were in school. Every girl we approached shot us down, and so we cheered ourselves up by going to McDonald's and buying ourselves some Happy Meals.

At about three o'clock I decided to make my way home so that I could walk through the door at around the same time I normally did on a school day. The last thing I wanted to do was to raise my parents' suspicion by coming home much later than I normally did. On the way home I stopped at a park near my house to change back into my uniform. I hid in some bushes so that no one would see me changing, and then once I was fully dressed I put my backpack over my shoulders, tied my shoes, and walked to my house as if I hadn't just skipped a day of school and used a park as a dressing room. When I walked through the front door my mom immediately called me into the kitchen. I stopped in my tracks. *The school didn't call did they?* You normally had to miss multiple days before the school called your parents. If you only missed one day the most they would ask for was a note from your parents explaining your absence.

With my heart beating and my stomach turning I walked slowly toward the kitchen. As usual, my mom was over the stove making the evening meal. As she heard me walk in she turned and said, "How was school?"

I swallowed hard. "It was fine, nothing special."

I waited for her to hit me with the news that the school had already called and that she knew I hadn't been there all day, but she didn't. She just turned back to the stove and kept cooking. I slowly backed away from her, made my way out of the kitchen, and ran upstairs. As soon as I got into my room I dove on the bed, buried my face in the pillow, and let out a big sigh. My heart was still racing, my palms were sweaty, and I was expecting my mom to come upstairs at any moment and rip me apart. But that never happened.

I had skipped school and gotten away with it. I'd outsmarted my teachers and my parents; I felt a sense of power. Armed with that feeling, I soon made a habit of that behavior and began to skip school at least twice a week. I always brought in a note that one of the older kids from my neighborhood forged to give to my teachers. My teacher assumed that there were some family issues going on at home because prior to this phase I had always been punctual. She never really dug much deeper into my absences at the time.

It's amazing that these same temptations had always been in my immediate environment but because I was working toward a dream I had never acted on them. It was only now that the dream was over, or at least on hold, that I began actively pursuing and engaging the temptations I had once resisted. When you have a goal you're working toward it is very easy to block out negative distractions. As soon as you stop having a goal every distraction becomes appealing. That's what I learned in my teen years, and as I gave in to my distractions more and more I made some decisions that led me on a downward path that severely threatened to end my football career before it had even started.

CHAPTER 4

MOPEDS AND BAD DECISIONS

It is not in the stars to hold our destinies but in ourselves.

—WILLIAM SHAKESPEARE

In today's society we often hear about how important it is to work toward a goal, a vision, or a dream. This message is preached daily to individuals, to businesses, to sports teams, and to Fortune 500 companies. We are told that we should have a goal because it gives us something to aim for and work toward. We are told that having a goal gives us a reason to be motivated, driven, passionate, and focused. In my own life I've found this to be true.

I've found that I'm always more motivated to do what I am doing if I have an end goal in mind. When you're working toward a goal or a vision it brings meaning to the process. Working with an end goal in mind gives you a reason to do what you are doing. If you're doing something with no end goal in mind it can feel like you're just going through the motions. I have been playing football since I was five years old and I've played on many different teams during that time. In my experience the most successful teams I have been a part of are the teams that had clear goals in mind at the start of the season. When a coach communicates a vision to his players it brings focus and unity to the whole team because they now have a common goal that they are all working toward as a group. Individually, each player is also clear on what role he needs to play to make sure that the team achieves its goal.

I've always found it very helpful when my coaches sat the team down at the start of the year to tell us what the goal for our season was. Once the end goal had been set we knew why we were practicing hard every day and why we were making the sacrifices that we did. Professional athletes spend a lot of time away from their families. During my career I seemed to always be on yet another flight or at a different hotel every week. That sacrifice is what you sign up for when you pursue a career in professional sports. And while it's never easy to be away from your family every few days, if you know why you need to be away it makes it a bit easier to handle.

Knowing the end goal always allowed me to understand why I had to do all of the things that I did. Playing games, practicing, travelling, and sitting in video meetings were just a part of the process toward that end goal. Trust me, if athletes don't know why their coach has them working hard and running at practice every day it won't be long before they lose enthusiasm and start asking themselves questions like, "What's the point of all this hard running?"

When there's no goal in mind there's really no reason or meaning behind anything we do. Having a goal allows you to understand why you do what you do, and this is true not only in sports but also in life. Can you imagine watching a football game where there was no goal for the teams to shoot at? Or a basketball game where there was no hoop? The players would be running around sweating and using all of their energy, but it would be for nothing because there'd be no goal for them to aim at or shoot for. That's how some of us go through life. We have no goal in mind and so we wake up, get dressed, go to school or work, use our energy, spend our time, and then come home at the end of the day and have no idea why we did any of the things we spent our day doing. We're playing football with no goals. We're running around using all of our energy, but at the end of the day we never actually score in life because we aren't aiming for anything. To win you have to score, and to score you have to shoot at something. If you aren't shooting for anything in life you'll never score.

Another reason you want to have a goal is because having a goal helps you to avoid distractions. When you know what you want to accomplish it becomes very easy to say no to temptations and distractions that try to take you away from your goal. Like I mentioned, when I was a young kid playing for Arsenal I was so focused on my goal of becoming a professional that I could easily say no to all of the distractions that tried to take me off course. It was my goal that kept me on the straight and narrow.

After leaving Arsenal I stopped dreaming and having a goal. I still played football here and there but I was just going through the motions. The passion, determination, hunger, and desire that I once had were all gone. I no longer had a big goal that I was aiming for, and if having a goal helps you to avoid distractions by making it easy to say no to them, then not having a goal makes it very easy to say yes to those very same distractions.

Without a goal I was powerless to say no to a lot of bad opportunities that came my way. One of those opportunities almost ended any chance I would ever get to play football professionally. I remember it as if it just happened yesterday.

It was June 2003. I was fifteen years old. School was winding down for the day and I was in class chitchatting with some friends as we waited for the final bell. It had been a really hot day, the kind that zaps all of your energy and makes a classroom the last place you want to be. We couldn't wait for school to be over so that we could go and make the most of this sunny day by doing the things we actually wanted to do.

With just a few minutes of class left one of the kids I was talking to told a group of us that he had stolen a moped earlier that day. He'd taken it from a busy street on his way to school and hidden it in some bushes in the park right behind one of our school buildings. This type of thing was common back then, and a lot of my friends from Tottenham either owned or regularly drove mopeds. A few even went one step further and owned cars or motorbikes.

Hardly anyone I knew had a legal job or the money to buy a moped, so you can probably figure out how they were able to get their hands on them. My guess is that they either stole them from people or used drug money to buy them, but regardless of how they got them, I saw a lot of my friends speeding in and out of the neighborhood all day and night in their biker jackets and helmets. I guess that's why it was no surprise to me that one of my fifteen-year-old classmates was capable of stealing a moped and then hiding it in a park.

Once the bell rang my friend took us to the bush that he had hidden the moped in. Despite all the mopeds that were around me, I had never actually ridden one before. I'm not quite sure why that was, but on this afternoon, once I saw all of my friends riding this thing around, I knew that it was time for me to get my first taste of riding a moped. We pulled the moped out of the bush, turned it on, and rode it to a street a few blocks away from the school. There were five of us taking turns riding. The other four had previous riding experience and seemed to know what they were doing right off the bat. When my turn finally arrived I put down my backpack, tightened my shoelaces, and hopped on the moped. I had no helmet and no license but I didn't care. Everyone else had ridden it and I couldn't allow myself to be the boring one out of the group.

I got the hang of it pretty quickly and before I knew it I was maxing out at fifty miles per hour up and down the street. Every time I drove by my friends they were egging me on as if I needed any extra encouragement to keep going. It was very stupid for me to ride a moped without a helmet and to be going in and out of cars at that speed on a back street where most people drove at twenty-five miles per hour, especially since it was my first time. But at the time all that mattered to me was proving to my friends that I could ride just as well as they could and that I wasn't scared to live life on the edge.

We rode on the streets for about an hour, and then we took our show to a local park. Since it was a hot summer day, there were a lot of people in the park having picnics and playing football. We were the center of everyone's attention as we recklessly rode around yelling and screaming as we went by.

After another hour one of the other guys suggested that we call it a day. It was getting dark, we'd had our fun, and so far we hadn't gotten into any trouble for stealing the moped or for riding without licenses and helmets. It was time to end our fun before anything went wrong, he said. Everyone else in the group agreed except for one person. There was one person who wanted to keep on riding for a little bit longer. That one person was, you guessed it, me.

I insisted that I needed to have at least one more ride around. "Just one more," I pleaded with the guys. I couldn't have known it right there and then, but that decision was about to alter the course of my life forever. We took the moped out of the park and back onto the street where we had began. As I climbed on the moped and sat on the seat I turned to my friends and smiled before telling them that I was just going to ride around the block one time before returning and calling it a day.

I revved the engine a couple of times and took off. What came next is a bit of a blur. I remember losing control almost as soon I started riding. I desperately tried to regain control but I started veering to the left. By the time I saw the car in front of me it was too late for me to try and avoid a collision. Crash! Bang! And then silence. Total silence.

The earth stopped spinning. Everything was happening in slow motion. I was lying on my side; my right leg was stuck between the concrete ground and the moped. It took all of my strength to push the moped off my leg as I tried to free myself. I wasn't feeling any pain. I looked up and saw that my friends were standing about ten feet away from me, so I decided to stand up and walk toward them. Their faces were expressionless and they were completely silent. The only sound I could hear was the sound of the evening traffic.

Now that the moped was off me I was able to get up and begin walking toward my friends. I put my left leg down first, and then I used the car I had hit to help me get up the rest of the way as I placed my hands on the bumper and pulled myself up. When I tried to put my right leg down so that I could stand I collapsed to the floor. My leg felt like jelly. There was no strength from the knee down and I wasn't able to stand up, but I still didn't feel any pain. Everyone rushed to my side. "Are you okay?" "Where does it hurt?" "Hang in there, Steve, we will call for help."

I had no idea what kind of damage I had done to my leg, but something was obviously wrong since I couldn't even stand up. I was, however, fully aware of the damage I had done to the car I had smashed into because the owner came over and started yelling at my friends and me. I can't remember exactly what he said but he clearly wasn't happy. His passenger door had a massive dent in it, so I guess he kind of had a right to be mad. A couple of people tried to calm him down, but he was going crazy, remonstrating with them as his arms flew wildly at his sides.

He got louder and louder until out of nowhere a young black lady came running out of her house and confronted him. She got right up into his face. "Can't you see he's hurt and in pain? Your car can be fixed, he's more important than a car!" She was yelling at him even more than he'd been yelling at me! This lady was like an angel to me, and after getting the angry man to calm down she went inside her house to grab me a blanket and a pillow, and she called me an ambulance. She assured me that she would stay by my side until the ambulance came. I thanked her for being so kind.

She then took her phone out and handed it to me because she wanted me to call my parents to let them know what had happened, but I politely declined. There was no way I was going to call my parents and tell them that instead of going straight home from school I had ridden a stolen moped for two hours without a helmet or a license, and that I was now lying on the ground with an injured leg because I had crashed it into a car. If I had told them that there would have been a funeral for me the following weekend.

I had done some bad things in my life, but this was definitely the worst. "You need to call your parents," she insisted. I could see that she wasn't going to give in until I did, so I took the phone from her and slowly dialed the numbers to our home phone. With every ring my heart rate increased. With my hand shaking I decided that I would lie about what had happened. I just couldn't bring myself to tell my parents the truth; I was too ashamed. And I figured that since I was going to speak in French to whoever answered the phone the nice angel-lady would have no idea what I said. It was my mom who answered.

"Where are you?" she questioned.

I told her the truth and said, "I'm with my friends."

"Well it's getting a bit late and you haven't been home since you left for school this morning and I'm about to serve dinner."

"Mom, I won't be home for dinner tonight."

I could sense her confusion through the phone, "Why not?"

I lied and said, "Well, I've been in an accident. Don't panic. I'm okay. A car hit me as I was crossing the road and now my leg is in a bit of pain, but I'm okay. I just need to go to the hospital."

She panicked. "What! Are you serious? What hospital are you going to?"

"North Middlesex."

"I'll meet you there. I'm going to tell dad."

I hung up and smiled at the lady as I returned her phone to her.

"You told her what happened?" she asked as she smiled back at me

"Yes, I told her everything," I replied, lying once again.

As I waited for the ambulance to come I passed the time by talking to my friends. A crowd had gathered by now, and I was starting to feel a throbbing in my leg. I could feel the pain begin to intensify in and around my knee. The sun was setting and a cool breeze was passing through the evening sky. With every passing minute the pain increased. I tried not to let the pain show on my face as I kept talking to my friends. In the distance an ambulance could be heard approaching as the siren blared out and the tires screeched at every turn.

In a moment of reflection I closed my eyes and began to think. A year ago I was playing for the Arsenal academy, dreaming of one day making it all the way to the first team. One year ago I had dreams of one day running out onto the pitch in front of the Arsenal fans. That dream was now nothing but a distant memory as I lay on the cold concrete ground with my head on a pillow and a blanket over me. My right leg was starting to hurt in ways I never knew it could. I couldn't walk, I had badly damaged someone's car, and I had lied to my parents about what had happened. I had never been to rock bottom before, but this place I was currently in couldn't have been far from it.

Later that evening as I woke up from a nap on my hospital bed my mind was overloaded with a million thoughts. The pain had subsided once my pain meds had kicked in. They made me feel extremely drowsy, but that was a small price to pay for a pain-free leg. The television was playing softly in the background. Nurses were going around checking on the different patients and attending to their needs. I had a couple of wires attached to me, and right by my head there was a monitor displaying my heart rate and some other information.

I replayed the day's events in my mind. *Just one more ride!* It's always that last one that gets you, huh? I couldn't help but feel that I had messed up big time and that my life as I knew it was pretty much over. My parents were at my bedside and so were two policemen. They had been standing there waiting for me to wake up from my nap because I had fallen asleep almost immediately after arriving at the hospital. The cops only had one question for me when I finally came around. They wanted to know if I was the kid who had crashed a stolen moped in Tottenham earlier that afternoon. I stared at them blankly before lying to their faces by telling them that I wasn't.

"Are you sure, young man?"

"Yeah, I'm sure. A car hit me," I said, trying to mask my trembling voice.

The officer leaned in and said, "Someone matching your description crashed a moped in Tottenham earlier today. Apparently, they were taken to a local hospital. You sure that isn't you?"

"Yes, officer, I'm sure. A car hit me as I was walking. I've never ridden a moped before."

"Okay, then. Sorry to bother you."

"No problem."

"Good luck with your recovery, mate."

"Thanks."

I had already lied to the to angel-lady, the doctors, and my parents (even though my dad immediately saw right through it), so I had left myself little choice but to continue with my story when the cops questioned me.

My dad had grown suspicious when I wasn't able to offer an explanation for the moped found at the scene. He wasn't someone who could easily be lied to and he was able to quickly piece together what had really happened. He never came out and said it directly, but just from the tone of his questions I knew that he knew I was lying. And he knew that I knew that he knew I was lying. We were the only two who knew. Thank God my mom and the nurse were in the room when he began his interrogation because they kept him from going any further by telling him that I needed my rest. As far as I was concerned, until he came out and publicly called me out for lying, my story was that a car had hit me and that was the story I was sticking to.

Not long after the cops left the doctor came in to check on me. His diagnosis was simple. I had torn some ligaments in my right knee, and I had also suffered some nerve damage, which would affect the sensation in my right foot. He thought it was best to operate that night so that I would give myself the best chance at a full recovery. My recovery was already going to be a long process, so he wanted to get me started right away. The doctor told me to rest a little bit more and then he would send someone to come and take me to the operating room.

I felt tears come to my eyes as I lay my head back on my pillow. I took a deep breath and began having flashbacks: *Just one more ride! Crash. Bang. I try to stand but I can't. My right leg feels like jelly, so I collapse to the floor. Angry driver starts yelling at me. Black lady makes him shut up. Ambulance arrives. Cops question me. I lie to cops. I lie to doctors. And I lie to my parents. Dad doesn't buy my story. Doctor says I need surgery. Rehab will be a long process.* All of these thoughts are rushing through my mind and there's no way I can stop them. There was no doubt that this was going to be a defining moment in my life, the most defining one thus far. The last thing I heard before I went to sleep was my dad asking the doctor when I would be able to start playing football again.

After Arsenal had released me I had gone to play for a team in the lower divisions called Leyton Orient. They were nowhere near as good as Arsenal, and the demands made on me there weren't nearly as high as they had been at Arsenal either. This suited me perfectly because since leaving Arsenal I had lost the desire to put in the work that was needed to become a professional footballer. I played for Leyton Orient because it was a way for me to make everyone think I still cared about football in the way that I once had. I felt that if I had just stopped playing football altogether after Arsenal had released me I would have looked like a quitter, like someone who gives up on their dreams easily, and that people would talk bad about me.

So even though I no longer enjoyed playing and I was way more interested in other things at that point in my life, I decided to keep playing football to make others think that I was still on the path to becoming the pro I'd always said I'd be. By playing at Leyton Orient I was also making my dad happy, because he still wanted me to play professionally one day.

Another reason playing at Leyton Orient suited me perfectly was because the level of competition was much lower than it had been at Arsenal. I never had to push myself to work as hard as I had done at Arsenal, so I was able to kind of just cruise along doing just enough to get by. If I'd been on a team that demanded me to really push myself I wouldn't have lasted a week because my desire to work hard at my game had completely gone. I was playing football for appearances sake and not because I was still chasing my dream. I was playing for all the wrong reasons.

After pausing to take in my dad's question, the doctor turned around, and with a look of confusion on his face, he replied, "Play? We are just going to try to get him to hopefully walk again." The injury was bad enough to put any hopes I had of ever playing again in the balance. Playing football again was a distant hope. My main goal would be to just try and walk properly again.

I required two surgeries, one for my knee and one to reattach the nerves that controlled my right foot. I had developed something called "foot drop", which basically meant that I had damaged the nerves that were responsible for the function of my right foot. They no longer worked, and so my foot just hung there, pretty much dead and of no use. I couldn't move it up or down or side to side, and when I walked it just dragged along the ground. No matter how hard I concentrated and willed it to move my foot never responded. The doctors were hoping that the second surgery I'd had, the one that had tried to correct my nerves, would eventually pay off and the function would return, but there were no guarantees. It was fifty-fifty whether or not I would ever fully regain the feeling in my right foot. That was certainly not the kind of injury that someone whose dream depended on the abilities of his feet would want to have!

I was discharged from the hospital a couple of days after my second surgery and my leg was put in a cast. The doctors told me to get started with my physical therapy right away in order to give myself the best chance of a full recovery, so I lined up weekly appointments with a local physical therapist.

In the weeks that followed my accident and subsequent surgeries I cried a lot. At first I cried because I began to really miss being able to play football. The lack of drive and passion that I'd experienced since leaving Arsenal was now replaced by a burning desire to return to the pitch. It's as if being physically unable to play had somehow rekindled the love I used to have for the game of football by showing me what I was missing. I resented being injured, and I was sick of the cast on my leg and my limited mobility. All I wanted was to be free to run around the pitch because it had always been my escape from all of life's problems. I could be having the worst day ever—I may have failed a test at school or had an argument with a friend—but as soon as I got onto a football pitch I would be able to push my bad day aside and find freedom and enjoyment from simply playing the game. I missed that a lot.

I also shed a lot of tears because I was slowly realizing that I had messed my life up. I was realizing that because of the decisions I had made I might never become a professional footballer. The worst thing about it all was that I was the only one to blame. No one had taken my dream from me; I had thrown it away. I had been blessed with talents and gifts that most people could only dream of, and rather than nurturing, developing, and refining these gifts I had abused and wasted them.

Life had given me the most beautiful gift I could have hoped for, but I had cheaply thrown it away as if it was just a gum wrapper or some junk mail. I hated myself for what I had done, and the tears kept on coming. I was now fifteen and I had no idea what I was going to do with the rest of my life. My identity had been stripped from me, and I was haunted in my sleep by the words that the doctor had spoken, "He needs to focus on simply walking again and not on playing football."

If I wasn't a footballer, who was I? I had no idea. This was the hardest thing I had ever been through. It was harder than being released by Arsenal and it was harder than being the outcast in my class when I first moved to London with my family. I was crushed, lost, and defeated. It had taken a serious injury to make me realize that my biggest passion in life was playing football and that there was simply nothing else that I wanted to do for a living later in life. It's as if I had to lose everything football represented in my life—my passion, my identity, my escape— in order to realize how much I really loved it. The moped accident and the double surgery were a constant reference point for me as I tried to recover from the broken leg I suffered in Colorado in 2011. There were some eerie similarities between the two incidents:

- Both injuries were to my right leg.
- Both injuries led to nerve damage that complicated my recovery.
- Both injuries required multiple surgeries.
- Both injuries left me unable to play football for over a year.
- Both injuries helped me to become a stronger person.

Being able to draw on my experience of having overcome a major injury once before was an invaluable resource for me to have in my fight to overcome my broken leg. I've often been asked which of the two injuries was more difficult to deal with and I've always answered that the first one, the moped one, was the harder injury to recover from. The reason is simple: when I got injured on the moped I hadn't achieved my dream yet. I was only a teenager and the future was a big mystery. I had to contemplate a life in which I might never recover from my injuries and never get to play football professionally. My broken leg, although it brought its own set of challenges, was slightly easier to deal with than the moped injury because I was already on the other side of my dream. I had already made it. No matter what happened with my rehab I could always look back and say that at least I had been able to achieve my dream of playing and scoring goals in front of thousands. It was by no means an easy injury to come back from but it was easier to deal with than the knee injury I suffered at fifteen.

If any good came out of my moped episode it was that my determination to get better and play again was at an all time high. If I never became a professional footballer I wanted the reason to be that I wasn't good enough, not that I had crashed a stolen bike and never recovered. My desire to get better stemmed from wanting to give everything I had to my dream.

Another reason why I so badly wanted to get better was that I was dying to get my leg out of the cast it was in. It was summertime when I got injured and the weather was really hot. The hotter it was the more my leg would sweat inside that massive, immobile cast. I would lie on the hospital bed, and later on my bed at home when I was discharged, trying to distract my mind so that I wouldn't think about my lower leg, which itched like crazy. I had no way of reaching my hand down into the cast to scratch it. All I could do was lie there and wish the itch away, but of course that never worked.

At times I would find a long stick or a long ruler and try to scratch my way to relief, but that seldom worked because I could never find quite the right angle from which I could directly attack the itch. It was a helpless situation and I spent many nights tossing and turning trying my best to fall asleep because that was the only way I could escape my ordeal. It was right then and there on that hospital bed with my sweaty, itchy leg that I decided I would never ever ride any kind of motorcycle again. If riding a motorcycle was the cause of unscratchable, itchy legs, then I would just stick to cars when I was older.

I spent the whole summer of 2003 contemplating life. I was struggling with my identity, as I really didn't know who I was anymore. I didn't want to be known for anything other than being a footballer, but it was hard to feel like a footballer when I had no team and I couldn't even walk properly yet following my surgery. Leyton Orient had told me that I could return to the club after I had recovered, but in my mind I knew I wouldn't be going back there. I wanted to get healthy first, and then I planned to find a better team.

My final year of school was beginning in September, so I spent the month of August trying to find a new identity for myself. Was I what every other teenager in Tottenham seemed to be? Just another young kid lost in the wilderness of indecision with no real chance or hope for true success in life? I thought about my friends who sold weed and wondered if I should ask them to bring me into their business. They seemed to always be happy and have money, so I wondered if that would be a good way for me to stay busy while I tried to get my leg better. Although that lifestyle appealed to me I ultimately decided against it.

At the time I had started writing some music with some friends from my neighborhood, but I couldn't really see a future in that. I tried not to think about school too much because I had fallen so far behind. I had neglected it a lot when I was a star at Arsenal, and since I was so sure that I would make it all the way to the professional level school had become completely irrelevant to me. My teachers always described me as "intelligent but easily distracted." I couldn't disagree with that assessment. I wasn't a dumb kid. I knew how to read and write, and if I applied myself I could have been a star pupil, but the distractions that arrive at every teenagers doorstep proved too strong for me to ignore.

I had placed all my eggs in one basket, and now that I had thrown that basket away I was left with nothing. Plan A had failed and there was no plan B or C for me to fall back on.

In my adult life I've been invited into different schools, universities, churches, and business organizations as a speaker for many events. One of the things I often talk about is goal setting and how important it is to be working toward an ultimate purpose in our lives. I talk about how important it is to wake up everyday not simply to try and make a living but to try and make a difference. I always have someone like Nelson Mandela in mind when I talk about this.

Mandela is a man who was practicing law as a black man in an apartheid South Africa. That alone, being a black lawyer in a racist country, was enough to make him successful in the eyes of many. But there was something bigger calling him. He decided to use his background in law as a platform from which he could fight for his, and the rest of black South Africa's, human rights. His dream to see black people given equal rights forced him to leave the comfort of his successful day job and enter the uncertain, violent world of the fight for civil and human rights. This dream of his would eventually lead to him being imprisoned for twenty-seven years. He spent twenty-seven years of his life in confinement because he wanted to make a difference! While in prison he didn't stop. In fact, in the twenty-seven years he was away in prison his story became known all over the world, and other countries began to pressure South Africa to release him, which they eventually did.

After leaving prison he became the president of the country that had made him an outlaw and a prisoner for much of his life. Mandela went from the prison cell to the presidency! Even Hollywood couldn't have written that script.

People from all walks of life revere Mandela; his life and death touched millions of people all over the world. He is an example we should all look to when it comes to living to make a difference and not just to make a living. The law career would have made him a living, but the ultimate goal in his heart, a free and peaceful South Africa for all, made him a difference maker.

Mandela's life taught me that when you have a passionate goal that you are working toward not even prison can stop you. Adversity will only stop you if you don't have a goal. I encountered many adversities as I tried to get back on the path to my dream of playing football after my accident, some of which you'll read about in the coming pages, and I am convinced that the only reason I was able to eventually overcome them all was because at the back of my mind I was working toward an ultimate purpose—a goal.

No matter how far off-track I got I always knew where I eventually wanted to end up. This is why I often talk about goal setting when I address different audiences as a speaker. I know that having a goal is the best defense against giving in to adversity, and having a goal was the only thing that allowed me to get through all of the adversity that would come my way as I tried to overcome the knee ligament and nerve damage that had set my life back a few steps. When you have a goal in mind, like Mandela had, you will encounter adversity, and your only weapon against it will be to keep working toward your goal.

As the summer was ending and the start of my final school year was approaching I set my goal of becoming a professional footballer at the forefront of my mind. I decided to do all that I could to get back to being healthy so that I could start playing again. I was really determined to reach my goal, and it's a good thing that I was, because if I hadn't been, as soon as the challenges and difficult days that were ahead inevitably showed up I would have given up and quit.

I did physical therapy for about two months after my surgery, but after being frustrated at the slow progress I stopped going to my appointments. My foot drop was the biggest problem. I learned that nerves regenerate at a very slow pace; they regrow about one millimeter a day, so my foot was still dragging along the ground as I walked. Once I had ditched the cast and the crutches and was able to put my full body weight on my leg I was still limited in my mobility because my foot wasn't under my control. I couldn't lift it up or down, which meant I was unable to jog or run.

There were two reasons I decided to start doing my physical therapy at home rather going to see the physical therapist. First of all, there was nothing the therapist could do for my foot drop. It's not like he could make my nerves regenerate any quicker than they already were.

The second reason was the time and cost it required to attend my appointments. The clinic where I did my rehab was in a place called Stanmore, which was about an hour away from where I lived if I took the tube. It would have taken even longer if I had decided to take the bus. We were a one-car family at the time, and since my dad was usually using the car, my mom and I had no choice but to take public transportation to my appointments.

My mom accompanied me to all of my physical therapy sessions and we bonded a lot on those long tube journeys. She always did her best to keep my spirits up because she could see that I was having a hard time coming to terms with how I had messed up my life and potential football career. She walked with me, talked with me, and cried with me through it all.

There were small victories, like the day I finally ditched my crutches and the day I was able to walk up a flight of stairs again without holding on to the railings. But those small external victories paled in comparison to the internal turmoil I was experiencing. I never showed it much outwardly but inside I was hurting a lot during that time. I was restless at night and I became a lot more anxious than I had ever been. The anxiety came from knowing that I would be turning sixteen in a few months. It wasn't merely the fact that I was turning sixteen that made me anxious; it had more to do with what becoming sixteen represented.

Back in 2004 sixteen was the age at which you finished your mandatory schooling in England. American kids graduate high school at eighteen, but in England we do it at sixteen. The school system in England is very different from the American one. In England mandatory education begins in what we call primary school, and it goes something like this:

PRIMARY SCHOOL

AGE	GRADE
5-6	Year 1
6-7	Year 2
7-8	Year 3

PRIMARY SCHOOL

AGE	GRADE
8-9	Year 4
9-10	Year 5
10-11	Year 6

Once you finish primary school you go to secondary school, the equivalent of high school in the U.S., and that goes something like this:

SECONDARY SCHOOL

AGE	GRADE
11-12	Year 7
12-13	Year 8
13-14	Year 9
14-15	Year 10
15-16	Year 11

In Year 11, you take your final exams, which are called GCSEs, and then you graduate. At that point you have two choices: the first is to enter the working world and never study again; the second is to continue on with your education. Most kids choose the second option and decide to continue their education by applying for college. The terms college and university are used somewhat interchangeably in America, but in England there is a distinct difference between the two:

College is a prerequisite for university. You attend college once you have graduated from secondary school. You spend two years there studying and preparing for university. You go to college between the ages of sixteen and eighteen.

University, which is from age eighteen onward, is where you go after you have passed your college classes. It works in a similar way to American universities.

With that lesson on the English school system in mind, you can maybe understand why I was extremely stressed out when I was in Year 11.

I had crashed the moped when I was fifteen years old while I was in Year 10, and after academically wasting Years 7 through 10; I was too far behind to make up for everything in Year 11. I was going to finish school with terrible grades, which limited my chances of getting into a good college where I could continue my education.

And to make matters worse, sixteen is also the age at which you normally earn your first professional football contract. Since I had suffered my injury I had no hope of earning such a contract. I didn't have a team, and even if I did have one I wouldn't have earned a contract because I was still waiting for the nerves in my foot to regenerate before I tried to play again.

My future looked bleak; sixteen years old with no grades and no contract. I had no idea what I was going to do. When I was at Arsenal and playing well I never worried about not having the right grades to continue my education because I didn't even want to continue my education. I didn't think I would need my grades because I had always thought I would leave my education behind at sixteen in order to begin my professional football career. Thoughts of doing anything else in the working world had never crossed my mind. I was going to play football for a living, end of story. At least that was my plan before I decided to have "just one more ride" on that moped.

When I combined my terrible grades with the fact that I had no chance of getting a professional contract it began to look like I was going to be forced into the working world and that scared me to death because I didn't know how to do anything well aside from play football. I didn't want to stack shelves at that age or be a cashier.

A lot of my friends went into construction work if they decided to forego further education, but I had no interest in construction work. Not knowing what my future held left me feeling helpless and afraid because I had never struggled with thoughts like this before. I had always been in that rare group of people who have always known who and what they wanted to become one day. That was no longer the case; I was lost.

If we are completely honest, I think we can all admit that there have been times in our lives when we've suffered from a lack of motivation. Whether we are professional athletes, doctors, teachers, lawyers, housewives, students, or politicians, there are some days when we simply don't have the energy to approach our jobs enthusiastically. We get into a mundane routine and end up going through the motions rather than approaching the task at hand with passion and excitement.

Where we once woke up excited every morning, sometimes not even needing an alarm clock to get us up, we now roll over and become best friends with the snooze button as we dread leaving the bed for the day ahead. I've been there before, even in my football career.

Sometimes it lasts two weeks, sometimes just two days, but it's something that happens to almost everyone. I've read several autobiographies penned by some of the best sportsmen and women of our time, and they often talk about going through phases in their illustrious careers where playing the sport just wasn't fun anymore. Michael Jordan left the NBA to go and play baseball while he was still in his prime. He'd lost the motivation that used to make the grind of going through an eighty-two game season enjoyable. Landon Donovan, arguably the best footballer that the United States has ever produced, spoke about feeling burned out and lacking motivation when he took a two-month break from his career at the start of the 2013 MLS season.

There were times in my career when I would have a hard time getting myself motivated for training in the morning. I still enjoyed playing, and there was nothing else I'd rather be doing, but I got into a routine where I was operating on autopilot and not from motivation.

The first couple of times it happened I had a hard time snapping out of it, but as I became more experienced and mature I began looking deeply within myself to try and figure out why I had those moments and how I could snap out of them when they came. When I sat down and began to look within myself I realized that the way to snap out of that funk where you don't feel as motivated as you usually do is to go back and remind yourself of why you began doing what you are doing. You need to reconnect with why you began doing what you do in the first place. You have to remember the big picture, the ultimate goal that makes all the hard work, setbacks, and tough days worth it. You have to go back to how you felt on your first day on the job—whatever it is you do. The nerves, the excitement, the anticipation, and the sense of gratitude; you have to channel all of those sensations you felt when you first began and let them inspire you out of your lack of motivation.

A lot of teachers begin teaching because they want to make a difference in the lives of their students. They have a desire to inspire their students to achieve academic success, and sometimes they want to inspire their students beyond the classroom. The thought of being an inspiration to a student gets them out of bed day after day. But after going through years of the same routine—class, recess, tests, homework, midterms, class, field trips, homework, recess, pop quizzes, finals—the passion that they started with is sucked away until teaching becomes more of a job than a livelihood. When it becomes just a job you lose your passion. But if you approach it as more than a job, as an assignment to make a real difference in the lives of your students, you will always be able to draw on a passion and sense of purpose that pushes past fatigue and a lack of motivation. This applies to all of us regardless of what we do.

As soon as I realized that the way to overcome a loss of motivation is to revisit the reasons you began doing what you do in the first place I began to apply it in my own life. When I went through a bad run of form or my team had lost a couple of important games and it was a little bit harder to get out of bed in the morning I began reminding myself of why I had begun playing football. I thought back to those days on the school playground when I played with my friends or when I played on the street in front of my house for hours at a time.

In those days there were no fans, no stadiums, no paychecks, no fame, no nothing; all we had was the ball and our passion. It was in those days that I fell in love with the game, and it was in those days that I did what I did because I loved it. That's the thing you have to go back to when you are struggling to motivate yourself. Whether you're a doctor, lawyer, athlete, student, housewife, politician, or CEO, it doesn't matter; the best way to overcome a lack of motivation is to refocus on your passion—on why you got started in the beginning and where you ultimately want to end up.

I remember talking to a student one day about an upcoming exam that he was going to take. This kid was nervous and he was having sleepless nights because of this upcoming test. I asked him to tell me what he was studying to become and he told me that he wanted to be a doctor because he was passionate about bringing healing to the human body. I then told him to remember that he wasn't in school to take exams. I told him that no one was passionate about taking an exam (if you or someone you know is passionate about taking exams, then you both need your heads examined!). I told him that it was important for him to see his exams as a necessary step in the process toward a future career in which he would be engaging his passion as a doctor. "That exam next week is just a stepping stone to your ultimate goal," I told him. "Don't let the constant exams and homework drain your motivation, instead you should let the ultimate goal that you have of becoming a doctor, the one that led you to school in the first place, inspire and drive you to keep going in times of anxiety or a lack of motivation." This is something that I now do in my own life on a regular basis. I am constantly reminding myself of what it is that I am trying to accomplish in the next ten, fifteen, and twenty years of my life. This usually helps me to maintain my drive and motivation.

But back when I was fifteen and facing a bleak future, my motivation was at an all-time low. The fear of the future paralyzed me and I avoided thinking about my post-school life at all costs. Not knowing what I would be doing once I graduated from secondary school made me extremely uncomfortable.

The only reason I was able to overcome my fear of the future and achieve my dream is because a certain teacher stepped into my life and decided to help me. His name was Mr. Goodison and he helped me by instilling a love for reading in me. He helped me by showing me that if I began to read about the successful people I admired and wanted to emulate, I could learn how to become a success in my own right.

One of the great ironies of my life is that I grew up refusing to read my schoolbooks, or any kind of books for that matter. I had no interest in reading. I played video games and ran around the neighborhood getting up to no good. I considered those activities to be fun, whereas reading was something I found to be extremely boring.

Today I consider myself to be a pretty avid reader. In the last ten years I have read books and journals across every spectrum. I have read on business, philosophy, religion, relationships, sports, history, business, and politics. I've learned so much from these books that I credit them for much of the success that I've been able to achieve in my life. However, the genre that has most impacted me is autobiographies and biographies. I absolutely love autobiographies.

Good autobiographies and biographies are priceless because they take you on the person's journey—through his or hers highs and lows, mistakes, successes, failures, lessons learned, bridges burned, mountains overcome, and wisdom acquired—all without leaving the comfort of your couch.

Through a biography you get to learn how Abraham Lincoln failed over and over as he ran for various positions in government before eventually becoming one of the greatest presidents in the history of the United States. A biography allows you to read how Oprah Winfrey, who came from humble beginnings and suffered from low self-esteem, went and became the pioneer of one of the highest-rated talk shows of all time, and a billionaire. It's inspirational.

I've read Martin Luther King, Jr., David Beckham, Barack Obama, Michael Jordan, Mother Teresa, Mahatma Gandhi, Nelson Mandela, Malcolm X, Tupac Shakur, Richard Branson, Walt Disney, and many more influential figures who have shaped history in one way or another. The reason I love autobiographies so much is because they have a unique way of causing you to believe in your own capabilities. They produce a "well if he can do it, then so can I" mentality. And the "it" I'm referring to isn't money or fame, it's overcoming the rough hand that life dealt us.

Autobiographies are one of the best discoveries I've ever made because they are where I learned about leadership. Most of us would agree that some of those names I just mentioned are considered to be great leaders in their respective fields. We hold them up as models of success and leadership as we applaud them for what they have achieved and overcome. As I read their stories over the years something unique began to stand out to me. I started to realize that all of these great leaders had something in common. From Abraham Lincoln to Michael Jordan, every single one of these leaders had the same thing in common. What was it that they had in common? What did I see as I began to read their stories? Let me tell you:

When I read the autobiographies of some of the world's foremost leaders I was surprised to find that among them they had taken exactly zero classes on leadership. Zero! That really amazed me. The greatest leaders of all time had never formally studied leadership! How was that even possible? Every day we are bombarded with leadership seminars, conferences, and events that promise to make us into great, fearless leaders, yet the greatest leaders of our time were not products of seminars or conferences. If leadership wasn't something that was taught to these people, then how did they become leaders? That was the question that came to my mind as I was reading their stories and trying to figure out how I could be a good, successful leader. The answer was a lot easier to find than I had expected.

Every single one of the leaders whose books I read became a leader when they had an encounter with their destinies. They all had a moment in which life showed them what it was that they were really supposed to be doing. They were all going about their normal lives until one day life interrupted them and called them to do something else. When they responded to that call they became the leaders that we know today. They became leaders when they discovered their passion and started living by it. Here are some examples of what I mean:

Martin Luther King, Jr.

By the standards of the time in which he was born, Martin Luther King Jr. came from a pretty comfortable background. He graduated from college in 1948 and was undecided about which profession he should join. He thought about a career in either law or medicine but in the end he chose to join the Baptist Church and become a minister. While studying at the Crozer Theological Seminary in Pennsylvania he came across the story of Mahatma Gandhi, an Indian freedom fighter who had used nonviolent methods to fight the British. King became convinced that this method of nonviolence was the approach that was needed to fight for civil rights in the United States. Rather than enjoy a relatively comfortable life as a preacher King decided to be the one to inject the nonviolent approach into the Civil Rights Movement. He was one of the prominent figures at the Montgomery Bus Boycott, where he was arrested for starting a boycott. Shortly after the boycott he was elected president of the Southern Christian Leadership Conference, an organization that was committed to using nonviolence as its main weapon. Its motto was "Not one hair of one head of one person should be harmed." This thrust him into the national spotlight and he became the leader of the entire Civil Rights Movement. He never sought leadership, he just responded to the call of destiny and that's what made him a leader.

Richard Branson

A failing, dyslexic student, Richard Branson dropped out of school as a teenager because he wanted to start a business. Told by his teachers that he was destined to be a failure, Branson considered settling for a regular job like most people he knew, but he decided to start a business instead because he wanted to help people. The first business he started was a magazine for students. It was an instant success and he went on to start a helpline that students who were struggling with a range of issues could call. After the helpline he started a record company called

Virgin Records, which became a huge success. Since Virgin Records he has started an airline, a phone company, a soda company, a wedding dress company, multiples health clubs, a cable, and about fifty more companies. When he left school he said that all he wanted to do was provide a bunch of businesses that offered excellent value for money. The call of destiny for Richard Branson was to become a successful businessman who would provide services that enriched our lives. He never sought leadership; he answered the call and became a leader.

Mother Teresa

While teaching at an all girls' school called Saint Mary's High School Mother Teresa felt that her true calling was to help the poor. She decided to leave her teaching profession behind and move to India, where she could actively begin to help the poor. She arrived in Calcutta with the goal of bringing aid to "the unwanted, the unloved, and the uncared for." With this mission in mind she opened a school and established a home for the terminally ill in a run-down building that she convinced the local government to donate to her cause. As more donations began to pour in Mother Teresa's charitable activities grew at the speed of light. During the fifties and sixties she established a leper colony, an orphanage, a nursing home, a family clinic, and multiple mobile health clinics. In 1971 Mother Teresa traveled to New York City to open her first American-based house of charity, and in the summer of 1982 she secretly went to Beirut, Lebanon, where she crossed between Christian East Beirut and Muslim West Beirut to aid children of both faiths. In 1985 Mother Teresa returned to New York and spoke at the fortieth anniversary of the United Nations General Assembly. While there she also opened Gift of Love, a home to care for those infected with HIV/AIDS. Her simple decision to respond to the call of destiny made her one of the greatest leaders this world has ever seen. She never sought to be a leader, but she became one by doing what life showed her she should be doing. She could have lived a good life as a teacher, but being a servant to the poor was her destiny.

Leaders are those who respond to their destiny and pursue it. They don't seek leadership positions or followers; they just find their calling and live it out. Some people are born to play music, some to build amazing architecture, some to fly planes, some to build businesses, some to be athletes, and some to be teachers. Whatever it is you're born to do, I believe that you will become an amazing leader when you decide to do it. To me, leadership has very little to do with a title or a position; leadership is living out your passion and using it to help others. That's what qualifies someone to be a leader in my eyes. If you are able to inspire people, improve their lives, and enjoy what you do while you do it, you're a leader.

I was born to play football. I know I was. At fifteen, when I ran around and messed my leg up over the joy of riding my first moped, I had lost sight of my calling. It took Mr. Goodison and some books to open my eyes and show me that I was born to play football. As I battled to recover from the injuries sustained in that crash, and I struggled with coming to terms with how badly I had messed up my education and my potential football career, the biographies of these great leaders stepped in and began to show me that I still had the ability to play football, and that this ability would be a platform from which I could give back and help others. If it wasn't for Mr. Goodison's intervention I would have never gone to play in the U.S. and I would have never been the first overall pick in the 2009 Major League Soccer Super-Draft. This teacher is the man who caused me to give education and books a second chance.

Every single one of the great leaders I mentioned earlier had a moment in their lives in which their destiny revealed to them what they were capable of doing; my destiny moment was when Mr. Goodison challenged me to rescue my football dream and use the platform it would give me to make a difference in the lives of others.

CHAPTER 5

A TEACHER FROM JAMAICA

Change is hard because people overestimate the
value of what they have, and underestimate the
value of what they may gain by giving that up.

—JAMES BELASCO AND RALPH STAYER

There is a famous saying that a lot of African and Caribbean mothers like to tell their misbehaving children:

If you can't hear, then you must feel.

All it basically means is that if you don't listen to sound advice eventually you'll have to feel the consequences that result from ignoring that advice. My late teenage years were living proof that the saying is true. I had ignored a lot of sound advice from my parents and my teachers over the years, and now as I watched my life begin to unravel I began wishing that I could go back and take their advice.

I went to secondary school at Gladesmore Community School. In my first three years at the school—Years 7 through 9—I was a pretty well behaved student. I was well known around the school because I was the best football player and everyone knew that I played for Arsenal; they had also seen me playing a few games for our school team. In class I was talkative but I was never rude to my teachers, and I was generally well liked by them even though I could have been better about doing my homework. All of that changed when I got to Year 10.

Arsenal had released me and I was behind in my schoolwork. My motivation for being in class went downhill and that's when I began to skip class and break a lot of rules. I stopped following the dress code, and on the days I did make it into school I was never on time. My classmates and teachers were shocked by my transformation; right before their eyes I was going from a well-liked kid to someone who no one, other than those who were doing the same things, wanted to be around. I could feel myself changing but I felt powerless to stop it.

This rebellious streak was my way of deflecting the pain I was feeling from being released by Arsenal. There was no one I felt comfortable enough to talk to about my pain. I didn't want to make myself look weak and vulnerable, so my only outlet became the way I behaved at school. If there were some people who felt that I was just going through a bad phase that I would soon snap out of and were willing to give me the benefit of the doubt, all doubt was removed on a Monday morning just as the school day was beginning.

Aside from having to wear a school uniform, another rule in terms of dress code was that we weren't allowed to wear baseball caps or have our hoods on inside the school building. One morning as the bell rang and everyone started making their way to their first class of the day I found myself walking through the hallway with my New York Yankees baseball cap on. About fifty feet ahead of me I could see Mr. Surgrue walking toward me. We were going to cross paths in a matter of seconds. A year before I would have removed my cap at the mere sight of Mr. Surgrue because he was the one teacher that you didn't mess with. There had been many times in the past when I had seen him reduce students to tears just by the way he yelled at them. He was by far the most feared teacher in the school; no student ever dared to give him any attitude or backtalk. He was the kind of teacher who would make you feel as if you were doing something wrong just by the way he looked at you. He gave you the same feeling you get when you're driving and a cop is behind you. Even if your license, registration, and insurance are in order and you are doing the speed limit you still get a little bit nervous anyway. That's the kind of feeling Mr. Surgrue gave the students. So no matter who you were you just didn't argue with this man. When he got to within ten feet of me he looked directly at me and began walking toward me. I kept walking with my cap on.

"Are you forgetting something, young man?"

I replied, "No," even though I knew exactly what he was getting at.

"We have rules in this school and you have been here long enough to know them."

"I'm not breaking any rules," I said defiantly.

"This is Gladesmore. We are not in New York, so take your cap off." His tone was getting sterner.

"I come to school to learn. My cap doesn't stop me from learning."

A look of complete surprise came across Mr. Surgrue's face. He was clearly in disbelief. No student had ever answered him back.

"Young man, I will not ask you again. TAKE YOUR CAP OFF!" I could see the veins in his neck bulging.

"No. And don't yell at me." I could hardly believe the words that were coming out of my mouth.

He took a step toward me and said, "You are going to get yourself into serious trouble if you keep going where you're going."

"I just wanna go to class."

"You'll be going home if you don't take that cap off. You are REALLY BEGINNING TO TEST MY PATIENCE. TAKE YOUR CAP OFF, STEVE!" The man was seething. He was foaming at the mouth and breathing heavily. His eyes pierced through me.

"NO." I had no idea why I yelled back, but I did. I wasn't in control of myself.

A crowd consisting of other students and teachers had gathered by now. Do I really want to go down this path, I thought to myself. I knew that there was no way of avoiding serious repercussions if I kept this up. Mr. Surgrue took another step forward and reached for my cap. I instinctively swerved and moved back. It was a move that wouldn't have been out of place in The Matrix!

"IN THIS SCHOOL THERE ARE CERTAIN RULES THAT WE FOLLOW! YOU ARE BREAKING ABOUT THREE OF THEM RIGHT NOW!" His voice shook every classroom door along that hallway.

"HOW AM I BREAKING THREE RULES? WHAT THREE RULES?" Did I really just yell back at Mr. Surgrue again?

"NUMBER ONE, YOU ARE WEARING A CAP INDOORS. TWO, YOU ARE LATE FOR CLASS. AND THREE . . ."

He took yet another step toward me. He was now within inches of my face,

". . . THREE, YOU SHOULD NEVER . . . EVER . . . NOT EVEN IN YOUR WILDEST DREAMS TALK BACK TO A TEACHER. ESPECIALLY NOT TO ME!"

His face was red with anger. He was breathing as if he'd just completed a marathon. My heart was racing and my stomach turned. I felt cornered and anxious. I was a rebel, but even rebels have their limits. I knew that it was time to stop. I stared him dead in the eyes as a way to cover up my fear. And then I took a step back and took my cap off. I walked away, and because of the other students present I pretended to look happy about what I had done, even though inside I was regretting every last word I had said to Mr. Surgrue.

For the next few days I was the talk of the school. "Steve's crazy." "Did you see how he stood up to Mr. Surgrue? That was amazing." But rather than feel a sense of pride at what I had done, I felt afraid. I was afraid that I was becoming someone I didn't recognize, and I feared that if I could have a public shouting match with Mr. Surgrue, then who knew what else I was capable of doing. I needed someone to step in and knock some sense into me. Thankfully, I wasn't the only one who was thinking along those lines. Mr. Goodison had been standing in the crowd watching me go at it with Mr. Surgrue, and after witnessing that event he decided that he needed to intervene in my life before I sunk to even lower depths.

Where I went to school we were conditioned to not like our teachers. Teachers were the bad guys. They were there to discipline us with their strict rules, and so we didn't like or trust them. We wanted to have fun in school and teachers, as far as we were concerned, were the fun police. They existed for the sole purpose of making our lives a living misery. That was the reality of life at my school from the students' perspective. But to every rule there is an exception, and if teachers being disliked was the rule, then the exception was Paul Goodison.

Mr. Goodison was a Jamaican PE teacher, who I met when I first enrolled at Gladesmore. I was in Year 7 and he was my PE teacher. Within a few days of being at my new school I immediately began to notice that he was held in high esteem around the entire school. All of the older kids spoke really highly of him; the guys respected him and the girls thought he was attractive. It didn't take me long to see why he was so well loved and celebrated. There were three specific reasons why he of all the teachers was the one who was well liked.

First, Mr. Goodison was a better football player than ninety-five percent of the students. This was a crazy thing to me because every other PE teacher I'd ever had didn't actually know how to play football well. They could teach it well, but they weren't capable of playing it well enough to keep up with the best players in the student body. We were normally too fit and too talented for our PE teachers. Mr. Goodison, though, was an exception. And not only could he keep up with us, he could also outplay most of us, or should I say, most of them; I mean he was good, but he wasn't that good! The simple fact that he could play football so well earned him a lot of respect from the male students.

Second, he was in tune with our culture. I went to school in Tottenham, and as I've mentioned it was a very rough place at the time. Most of the adults either couldn't identify or couldn't relate to our culture. In Tottenham we only liked certain kinds of music, we spoke using certain slang terms, and we generally walked around with a chip on our shoulders because of the rough surroundings that we lived in. Mr. Goodison understood all of this. He could talk the latest slang and he knew the lyrics to the current songs we were listening to. Growing up, his background had been similar to ours and that allowed him to understand us better than our other teachers.

And third, from the very first day of class Mr. Goodison made it clear to all of us that he would not tolerate any rudeness, misbehavior, or attitude from any student. He warned us that there would be hell to pay for any student who decided to disrupt his class or refused to pay attention when he spoke. We Tottenham kids were tough; Mr. Goodison showed us that he was tougher. There were some students who didn't take his words at face value and decided to challenge him. They soon found out that he was definitely a man of his word. There was this thing he used to do to any student who wasn't paying attention to him when he spoke that scared us to death. Sometimes when class was over he would ask all of us to sit down in front of him so that he could recap the lesson from that day. As he stood over us talking he would always hold a ball in his hands, and then without warning he would throw the ball at full speed toward one of us. His logic was that if you were paying attention to him you would simply catch the ball and no harm would have been done. But if the ball smacked you in the face, well then, that just meant that you hadn't been paying attention to him otherwise you'd have seen it coming. He wanted us to pay attention at all times. It was an extreme method, to say the least, but he definitely had my attention any time he spoke. In those lesson recaps I never ever let my eyes wander to the left or to the right; they were always firmly fixed on Mr. Goodison. In the years he taught me I had to catch my fair share of balls. I have never played goalie, but with the amount of times I had to catch a flying ball from Mr. Goodison I think I received enough training to have become a pretty good one!

I had a good relationship with Mr. Goodison during my first two years at the school. We bonded over football more than anything because as well as being my PE teacher he also coached the school football team and I was his star player. I never gave him any problems and he always commented on how respectful I was to him. There were many bad students in the school, but in his eyes I was definitely not one of them. This was all true in Years 7 and 8 when Mr. Goodison taught me. But when I got to Year 9, without warning, Mr. Goodison had disappeared.

No real explanation was given as to why he was no longer at the school, but for the entire year that I spent in Year 9, he was nowhere to be seen. He was replaced in the PE department, the football team got a new coach, and life at school went on as normal. But just as suddenly as he had disappeared he reappeared again after being away for a year. We learned that he had taken a year off from teaching so that he could travel the world with his girlfriend. They had visited some countries that they'd always wanted to see like Thailand, Malaysia, and Singapore.

The first thing Mr. Goodison saw on his return to the school was my fight with Mr. Surgrue, and to hear him tell it, the Steve Zakuani who he saw when he returned from his travels was a completely different person from the Steve Zakuani he had left behind. He'd been standing in the hallway talking to another teacher when he'd heard a commotion coming from the other end of the hallway. He saw a crowd flocking toward the loud yelling, so he made his way over to see what all the fuss was about. When he got there he could not believe what his eyes were seeing: Steve Zakuani, little Steve who just loved football and was always so pleasant to everyone, especially to him, was standing there publicly arguing with Mr. Surgrue, of all people. Right away Mr. Goodison knew that something bad had happened within me while he had been away. And he also knew that if someone didn't step in and knock some sense into me I was on a fast track to failure.

In the time that Mr. Goodison had been away I wasn't the only who had changed. Mr. Goodison had changed a lot, too, and maybe even more than I had. Where he once dressed in casual sports clothes, he was now dressed in really smart business-like attire. He no longer walked with a sports bag; he now carried a briefcase and he hardly used any slang terms in his vocabulary. He no longer taught PE; he was now a math teacher. He had also lost a lot of weight because of a new diet that he was on. He had always been very muscular with a strong upper body, but he was now really slim and lean. His change was drastic.

Personally, I couldn't believe it. The new Mr. Goodison kind of freaked me out, so I decided that I would just stay away from him. No one really knew why he had changed so much and so suddenly, but within a few weeks of his return he invited a few students to join his new after-school mentoring program. I was one of only sixteen students that he had selected and it wouldn't be long before he revealed to us why he was a new man and how he could help us become new people, too.

"If you're here today, it's because I think you are in danger of failing your final exams at the end of next year, and that you will fail in life once you get out of here and into the real world . . . unless I help you." That was how Mr. Goodison opened up the first session of his mentoring program. *Gee, thanks! I'm here because you think I'm a failure,* I thought to myself. He had handpicked sixteen Year 10 students whom he felt were going to fail their final exams the following school year, in Year 11, the exams we took before graduating. Upon returning from his travels Mr. Goodison had made it his mission to not only help us pass our exams but to teach us life lessons that were not typically taught in the classroom. That was the whole premise of this new after-school mentoring program.

Over the next two years he planned to transform all sixteen of us from boys into men by teaching us life lessons in the areas of goal setting, financial planning, health and nutrition, manhood, and leadership. There was no official name for this program, but he began holding a meeting in his classroom every Wednesday at four o'clock. These meetings would prove to be revolutionary because nothing of this kind had ever been done in my school or in any school that I'd heard of. No teacher had ever taken the time to do something like this.

Once the bell rang at the end of the school day, rather than go home, we would make our way to Mr. Goodison's classroom to be mentored. The meetings lasted about four hours because no one wanted to leave. We had never been taught about any of these things and we wanted to soak it all in. Sometimes I felt as if we could have stayed there all night had it not been for the janitor kicking us out when it was time for him to lock up. The meetings were especially life changing for me because had it not been for them my life never would have turned around.

Everything I went on to accomplish in my life, from a successful college soccer career at the University of Akron to a successful MLS career (primarily before my injuries) to founding my own organization that has already helped thousands of people in many ways, I can trace back to everything I learned in those mentoring sessions.

After that initial first session I went to only about four more meetings for the rest of that first year. Part of the reason for that was that I was not in school very often, but it was also because the things that Mr. Goodison was teaching us were not suggestions or options; he was teaching us things that he believed we had to do in order to be successful in life. He saw the world in a very black-and-white way when it came to failure and success. Everything you did on a daily basis was either leading you to failure or to success there was no in between. His mentoring class wasn't designed to keep us in our comfort zone, it was designed to challenge us to make positive changes in our lives. I couldn't really disagree with anything that he was teaching us, because it all made perfect sense, but I feared that if I kept exposing myself to his teachings I would be forced to implement the changes he required into my own life. I would have to stop skipping class, I would have to stop being friends with the people who were leading me astray, I would have to stop cursing, I would need to start doing my homework, and I would have to stop being late to school.

Change is always uncomfortable, and I knew that making those changes would require me to start living in a completely new way, with a brand new mindset. I was scared to change. Even though I was headed for failure I was comfortable with how I was living. It was easy to show up late to school and not do my work once I was there. I didn't want to take the time to set myself lofty goals, create a vision for my life, and read books on business and leadership, which is what Mr. Goodison was challenging us to do. After deciding that I was not ready to change, I stopped going to his mentoring class and started avoiding him any time I saw him around the school building.

Mr. Goodison had grown tired of the same routine. He had been teaching PE for several years and it had gotten to the point where he simply needed something different. After sharing his frustration with his girlfriend, Michelle, he decided that he needed to take a year off from teaching so that he could travel the world and expand his horizons. With a backpack and a little bit of cash he set off for Asia.

On his travels he did a lot of reflecting. He thought about his life's journey up to that point and had long conversations with Michelle about the future. He couldn't explain why but all of a sudden he had this inner urge to do more and be more. He woke up each morning feeling as if he was living a life that was well below what he was capable of. Somewhere deep inside him he could sense that he had a lot more to give of himself than he had given thus far.

He had a great time experiencing the diverse cultures of places like Thailand and Malaysia on his travels as he enjoyed meeting the people and trying the different foods. With the freedom and spare time that came from not having to follow the schedule of a school day for the first time in years, Mr. Goodison spent a lot of time on the beach staring out at the ocean and thinking about his life.

One night as the sun was setting and the waves gently splashed in the background Mr. Goodison caught himself staring in wonder at the beautiful sunset before him. He realized that he had never actually stopped to admire something as simple as a sunset. He'd gotten so caught up in the busyness of life that he had never taken five minutes out of his day to just quietly admire a sunset. *When was the last time I just relaxed and enjoyed a sunny day? When is the last time I went to a concert? I've been teaching PE for so long, but is that what I want my legacy to be? I feel like I'm just teaching PE because it's all I've ever known. Am I really helping the kids as much as I can by just being their PE teacher? I can't even remember the last time I directly made a positive impact in someone's life.*

These thoughts ran through Mr. Goodison's mind that night and they led him to make the conscious decision that he would stop being so busy trying to make a living that he forgot to enjoy his life. He wrote down in his journal that he would spend the rest of his life helping people to live the best lives they could possibly live rather than living the lives that were expected of them, like he'd been doing. That's how the mentoring program was born. After that night Mr. Goodison began to read on any and every subject, as he wanted to be able to teach people how to achieve optimal health and success in mind, body, and spirit.

In the second year of the mentoring program, my last year of school,

I attended most of the sessions. My notepad was usually full from the notes I was taking as Mr. Goodison taught us everything he knew about success. As he paced the room delivering his presentation every single set of eyes followed him. You have to understand that the kids in this program were sixteen of the most unreachable kids in the whole school. We were the kids who were expected to fail. Most of our teachers had already given up on us and were counting down the days until we graduated and exited the school building forever. So the fact that Mr. Goodison could hold our attention for several hours with no disruptions was no small feat, especially when you consider that we technically didn't have to be there; it was after school hours and the program was optional.

If I had to name one reason why I thought his program was so successful, I would say that it was because of the content. What we were learning in this program was not something that we could go and get anywhere else. No school that I knew of had any classes that taught what Mr. Goodison was teaching. And if they did happen to have classes that taught what he was teaching, they definitely weren't capable of teaching it how he taught it. He was a phenomenal communicator. Here is a summary of what he taught us for two years:

VISION

He began by telling us that we needed to create a vision for our lives. He taught us that we needed to go through every day with an idea of where it was that we wanted to end up and what it was that we wanted to do. This would help us to maintain our focus through the many distractions of life.

GOAL SETTING

After he had helped us establish visions he told us to set goals that would help us get to those visions. He taught us how to set realistic yet challenging weekly, monthly, and yearly goals that we could use to measure whether or not we were making progress toward our visions.

HEALTH AND NUTRITION

To my sixteen-year-old mind Mr. Goodison ate a lot of weird stuff. He always brought his lunch to school in plastic containers, and any time I caught a glimpse of it I lost my appetite. I was used to eating burgers, fries, pizza, and chicken wings every day. Mr. Goodison ate a lot of greens, hummus, and fruit. He taught us that setting long-term goals was pointless if you didn't live long enough to see them. He told us that health was the key to a long life and maximizing our energies. We learned the importance of a balanced diet and an active lifestyle.

MANHOOD

Since the program was designed for boys, Mr. Goodison taught us all what a real man is supposed to be like. I would say that seventy percent of the kids in my school either did not know who their father was, or if they did they did not have a good relationship with him. We got our ideas of manhood from the examples we saw in our neighborhoods, and most of these were not good. Mr. Goodison taught us that a man was someone who took care of his responsibilities, always treated women with the utmost respect, was a hard worker, knew where he was going in life, and was law abiding.

FINANCIAL MANAGEMENT

This part of the program was simple. Mr. Goodison taught us to save more than we spent.

LEADERSHIP

Mr. Goodison's philosophy of leadership was that a leader is one who serves others. He taught us to use our gifts and talents to serve our communities and the world around us. He also taught us that leaders come in many different forms, that it isn't always the charismatic people who are leaders.

I'm naturally an inquisitive person. I like to ask why all the time. I was born with a desire to want to know the reason behind anything I am asked to do, and so I tend to ask a lot of questions in life. That's a small part of the reason why I've read so many books; if I have a question or I'm unsure about something, I read up on it. My questions never come from a malicious place, and I don't question things just to be a pain in the neck. I genuinely have a desire to know the reasons behind things.

This inquisitiveness was on full display in the mentoring program. With all of the new information I was learning I couldn't help but to challenge Mr. Goodison on some of his theories. "Why do I need to have a goal?" "What if I only do half of the things you're telling me, will I be a half-success?" "If God wanted us to eat healthy food, He would have made it taste better!" Over time he came to expect this from me and sometimes the sessions would turn into personal duels between him and me. We would go back and forth as my classmates watched in excitement and waited with anticipation to see what Mr. Goodison would say to finally shut me up. I found that no matter what I threw at him he seemed to always have an answer. I was a formidable opponent, but he always won.

Have you ever heard someone say something along the lines of, "It changed my life forever"? The "it" that they're referring to can be:

- a movie
- an inspirational speech
- meeting a personal hero
- witnessing a major event

I've heard people say things like, "That documentary I watched last week changed my life," "When I met that war hero and he talked to me about his life it changed mine forever," and "I attended a seminar and I heard this phenomenal speaker, she changed my life." We've all heard people make these kinds of statements, but I've always wondered whether one single event can really change your life. Can something you watch on TV change your life in an instant? I'm not sure that it can. I think what one single event can do is to spark in you the desire to make some changes. It can challenge or inspire you to change, but it can't change you. The war hero that you spoke to didn't change you, hearing his story made you want to change, but he didn't change you. He sparked in you a desire to change. Nothing can change us until we are ready to change.

I believe that there are certain events that happen in our lives whose sole purpose is to spark in us the desire to change. These moments are so profound that they force us to look at ourselves in a way that nothing else ever has before. And after taking a look in the mirror we begin to make adjustments. I experienced one of those moments that made me look at myself in a new way during the very last mentoring session that we ever had with Mr. Goodison. This moment was the first domino to fall in a series of events that led me down the path that got me to where I am today. It seemed insignificant at the time, but without it nothing else would have happened for me.

When I look back on my life I can clearly see that I've lived two very different stories. In the first half of my life I was my own worst enemy. I thought I knew what was best for me, but in reality I was headed for destruction. My disregard for authority figures like teachers, my desire to be friends with people who spent their day breaking the law, as well as my complete indifference toward my education, is a complete contrast to the person I've become in the last ten years of my life. Back then I never would have guessed that I would found an organization whose mission, among other things, was to educate people both academically and beyond. I didn't change overnight, my change took a while to come full circle, but the desire to make it happen was sparked in one moment.

It was my last week of school. All that was left after this week were my final exams. I was feeling good, not about the exams but about being done with school. In a few short weeks I would finally be free from the chains of education and I would be let loose into the adult world. Although the fear and uncertainty of what my next step looked like was very real—as I had no professional contract, and barring a miracle of biblical proportions I was going to fail most of my exams,—due to my excitement over leaving secondary school behind, I was able to push those fears to the background.

The only thing I was going to miss about school was Mr. Goodison's mentoring program. I felt a tinge of sadness as I walked into his class at four o'clock on the last Wednesday of my school career. His program had been a welcome distraction from the things we were normally taught in school and I had learned a lot about life.

In this last session, Mr. Goodison was talking to all sixteen of us about how we should take charge of our lives and stop being afraid to take risks. He was telling us that we shouldn't be imprisoned or limited by the opinions of others and that we needed to be the pilots of our own destinies. He told us that once we got out into the real world it would be up to us to go ahead and apply the things he had taught us. He warned us that life was hard and that we would make many mistakes. He ended his warning by telling us that the one mistake we should never make was the mistake of living a life that others wanted us to live.

"Live the life you want to live. As long as you don't break any laws and you are a positive example, live the life you desire!" We were all captivated by his words. *I am really going to miss this.* When we were in his sessions it never felt like we were in school. I used to get lost in the world he was describing, a world in which I was successful and a good example for others to follow. I longed for that world.

As he wound down the final session he began to tell us that even though we may have felt like we were, none of us were actually in control of our lives. He guaranteed us that there were areas in our lives that were being controlled by the opinions or wishes of other people and that until we realized this we would always be living to please those people. The clothes we wore, the music we listened to, and the way we thought, were most likely the result of other people's influence he told us.

He went on to explain that over time we had been influenced to fit in to what was considered normal and cool and that most of the decisions we made on a daily basis came from a place of trying to fit in rather than from a place of us doing what we actually wanted to do. This was brand new information for all of us. I had never even stopped to consider why I wore what I wore or did what I did from day to day.

I wanted to challenge him, but deep down I knew that he was right. I looked down at my feet and saw that I was wearing Wallabees. Every guy in the school, and even some girls, wore Wallabees. I can't remember how or why they became popular, but for a time Wallabees were the shoes to have. In terms of quality there were far better options. Wallabees only lasted about six months before the soles began to wear thin. In terms of price, they were more expensive than other, simpler (better) shoes I could have worn to school, shoes that would have lasted me at least two years. Despite their questionable quality and durability and their more expensive price, I still chose to wear Wallabees simply because they were in style. Everywhere you turned, kids were wearing them and I didn't want to be left out. It wasn't about getting the best shoes; it was about getting the shoes that would allow me to fit in. Mr. Goodison had a very good point.

Before he closed out our last ever session with him he announced that he had one more very important question to ask all of us. "Is there anyone in this room, anyone at all, who believes that they are in total control of their lives?"

Silence. Complete silence. I could see the trap that Mr. Goodison had laid out. He had posed the question in the hopes that one of us would answer "Yes", which would set him up perfectly to tell that person all the reasons why they were not in control of their lives. He had his argument lined up before he had even asked the question. I think the other students saw the trap, too, because no one made a sound. We could see that he was ready to prove us wrong.

I looked around and most of the students had their heads down, they were avoiding making eye contact with Mr. Goodison. Since I had spent half of my time in the mentoring program questioning and challenging him, I decided that I would do it one more time, for old times' sake. Did I believe that I was in total control of my life? No. Did I believe that the way I dressed, walked, talked, and cut my hair were not influenced by the latest trends and by a fear of not wanting to be the odd one out? No, they definitely were. Of course we are all influenced to dress a certain way, drive certain cars, and live in certain places. There's nothing wrong with that. But when we make lifestyle choices for the sake of fitting in or because we are too scared to just be ourselves, that's when there's a problem.

I raised my hand. I felt the other students turn to look at me as if to say, "What took you so long?" A wry smile came across Mr. Goodison's face. "Steve, I was expecting this," he said. And then he told me to stand up. I scooted my chair back and did as he had asked. The other students laughed quietly, they knew what to expect. The only two people standing in the room were Mr. Goodison and me; our final battle was about to commence.

"So, Steve, you're in control of your life, are you?"

"Yes, yeah of course I am," I confidently answered.

He smiled and asked, "Are you sure about that?"

"Yes, I'm sure. No one controls me."

"Really?"

"Yes, really. I do what I want."

He paused for a brief moment, and then he said, "Okay, well let me ask you a question."

"Okay."

"Do you like coming to school, Steve?"

In all my years at school, this was the easiest question I'd ever been asked. "No, of course not."

Mr. Goodison wanted me to confirm my answer. "You don't like coming to school?"

"No, sir. I hate school."

"Alright, okay. Well, then why do you keep on coming back?"

Without hesitation, I replied, "Because of my parents, they make me come."

"Oh, they make you come, do they?"

"Yeah, that's what I said. I come because they make me."

"So," he paused and looked around the room, "is it fair if I say that your parents control that area of your life then?"

"Huh?"

"Well, if you only come because of them, then they control the coming-to-school area of your life, right?"

Damn, he's got me, I thought. And then I said, "Right, yeah. I mean, no. I mean . . ."

I was speechless. The whole class laughed at me as I sat back down in my chair.

That night I tossed and turned as I tried to sleep. *Then your parents control that area of your life.* Mr. Goodison's words ran through my head all night. It wasn't what he had said that had left me restless. It was what he hadn't said that troubled me. He hadn't done an inventory of my life to show me all the different areas that were under the control of others, but I bet he could have.

And although I knew that going to school was an area in which I didn't have much of a choice I began to wonder about the other areas of my life in which I did have a choice. I wondered if I was in control of those areas. *Who controlled what I did with my free time? Who controlled the music I listened to and the things I watched on TV? Why did I dress the way I did? Was that my choice or was it someone else's? Was there anything I did simply because I wanted to do it? Or was my whole life the result of trying to fit in to what was expected of a teenager from a tough neighborhood like Tottenham?* I thought about the way I treated people, always harsh and putting on a tough front, trying not to show any signs of weakness. *Where had I learned this behavior? Isn't that how all the people I considered to be my friends treated people?* I thought about the way I approached my education. I was never on time for school, I routinely skipped class, I was lazy in my work, and I was extremely talkative in class. *Why was I behaving like that? I wasn't always this way, so where did I learn this? Isn't that the way my friends behaved?*

I sat up in bed and thought about my friends. Half of them had become parents before they were eighteen, and the other half had left school with terrible grades. Some of my friends were well-known drug dealers, while others were well known for being violent people in the community. It wasn't hard to see where I had learned to behave how I did. I wasn't in control of my life.

I realized that I wasn't happy and that I hadn't been happy in a very long time. I felt as though I had thrown my life away on that moped and rather than deal with the pain resulting from my actions I had buried them underneath a rebellious, loud, and confident persona that I displayed for others. Deep down, however, I had low self-esteem, and I was lost and miserable. I had lost my way a while back and I was now ready to admit that I direly needed help. Since my accident I hadn't kicked a football and I missed it terribly.

All the time I used to spend training and chasing my dream was now being spent with the wrong crowd, with people I had no business being around. I had even been kicked out of my parents' home for a few weeks after they discovered that I had been skipping school several times a week for the last few months. I literally slept on the concrete in front of my front door on that first night before I went and lived with a friend for the rest of my time away from home. Can you imagine living out of a backpack with a friend who wasn't much older than you during your final school exams? It's a miracle that I made it to the exam center at all on some days.

That night as I lay on my bed I knew that I needed to make some changes in my life. For the first time in my life I was ready to change. I wanted to change! My life had spiraled out of control and I needed to grab a hold of it quickly. The seed that would spark the change that took place in my life over the next few years had been planted. I would, however, require one more encounter before things really clicked and the change in my life accelerated.

CHAPTER 6

JUNE 12, 2005

A teacher affects eternity; he can never
tell where his influence stops.

—HENRY ADAMS

SEPTEMBER 2005

"You should really think about doing something else with your life because you will never be a professional footballer, I can just tell by the way you run."

Those were the words I heard back in the summer of 2005 when I was seventeen. I had spent a total of just one day training with Queens Park Rangers—a good team, but not a great team, and certainly not a team that I wasn't good enough to play for at the time, before one of their coaches told me that my running style would prevent me from ever having a career in professional football.

QPR were the fifth or sixth professional team I had tried out for in my attempted comeback from the injuries I'd sustained in my moped crash, and so far, despite doing all that I could to earn a professional contract—I had been to three different countries, staying in less than desirable motels and hotels—no team had wanted to sign me. Still, my fire was burning. I refused to let anyone or anything stand in the way of my dream. I will have a career in professional football; I have to. I didn't allow the rejections I experienced from Wigan Athletic (England), QPR (England), Real Valladolid (Spain), FC Top Oss (The Netherlands), and AZ Alkmaar (The Netherlands) to dampen my enthusiasm as I went about pursuing my goal. I was relentless in my pursuit.

Rewind thirteen months to August 2004. I'm lying on my bed at my parents' home in London. I feel like I haven't moved in three days. My motivation to get up and do something has hit an all-time low. It's been three months since I left school and fourteen months since my moped accident. My final exams didn't go too well and I failed classes that I would have easily passed had I bothered to study and do the work. Aside from English Literature and English Language, in which I got A's, the rest of my grades were less than what I was truly capable of. Because of that I wasn't exactly sure what my next step in life should be.

Continuing my education didn't appeal to me, and neither did getting a job. It had been over a year since I had played football, and I wasn't sure if I ever wanted to play again. It's not that I didn't miss playing football; God knows I missed it. But I knew that if I wanted to get back to playing at a level worthy of earning a professional contract I would have to put in a lot of work, more work than I had ever done before. And to be honest with you, I didn't think I had the desire or the necessary fight in me to do so.

In August 2004 I had no desire to put in the work needed to regain the fitness I had lost since the accident. I knew that I would have to spend hours in the gym re-strengthening my leg and conditioning myself if I wanted to try and pursue my original dream of being a footballer. I saw it as too much of a demand at the time; it was a price I was not willing to pay. A year later, in September 2005, I was in a different space. I was enthusiastically traveling across Europe trying out for different teams and putting everything I had into my dream.

So what happened between August 2004 and September 2005 that gave me a completely different outlook on trying to achieve my dream? What happened that caused me to do a complete 180? Well, it all began with a simple phone call.

Oscar was a friend I had known since I was eleven years old. We played together during my final two years at Arsenal and we had stayed in touch ever since. He called me one Sunday night in August 2004 because he wanted to invite me to attend a practice the following night for a new team that he had just joined. This team was brand new and it didn't even have an official name yet; a nineteen-year-old guy called Abbey Casal had started it.

Abbey started this team so that kids who hadn't received professional contracts would have a place to regularly play at a high level. He also planned to videotape all of the games that the team played so that he could send clips to professional teams around the world and to colleges in the U.S. to get his players some exposure. The plan was for the team to comprise of kids who were still hoping to play professionally one day, kids who had once been on professional youth teams but hadn't received professional contracts when they had turned sixteen.

In England most kids stop playing once they reach sixteen if they haven't already been signed to a professional team, so it was rare to find a competitive team that catered to those kids sixteen and older who still wanted to play for more than just leisure. That's where Abbey was unique; he was creating a competitive team that would allow aspiring footballers to keep playing and keep getting better while chasing their dreams. He was the only person I knew who was attempting to do something like this.

They were expecting to be low on numbers for their first ever practice session, and that's why Oscar had called me; he wanted me to help fill out the numbers. I told him I would be happy to come because it would be fun to play with him again, but when the day came I didn't go. I hadn't kicked a ball since I had gotten on that moped, and aside from the fear that I would get injured again I wasn't sure if I was still good enough to play and compete with kids who were passionate about the sport. I decided to spend my Monday night in bed watching television rather than going to this training session. Tuesday night brought another phone call.

"Steve, it's Oscar, where were you last night, man?"

"Sorry, man, I got busy with some stuff."

"Okay, no worries but we practice again tomorrow night. Can you come?"

I sensed in his voice that he really wanted me to come. "Maybe. I'm not sure yet."

"Well, we practice at 6 p.m. and I can have the coach pick you up near your house if that helps?"

"Umm, yeah, I guess that helps," I said, unconvincingly.

"Okay, he'll be at the train station near your house at 5:30 p.m. tomorrow."

"Okay."

"Make sure you come," Oscar pleaded.

"I'll try my best. I'll try."

We hung up the phone. I still had no real intention of going to practice the next day. I was just telling Oscar what he wanted to hear so that our conversation would be short. I felt bad that I had let him down the night before but not bad enough that I wouldn't do it again.

When Wednesday arrived I was in bed watching a movie when my phone rang. It was Abbey, the coach and founder of this new team. Reluctantly, I answered it. We talked for a bit and he told me that he remembered watching me play as a kid while I was at Arsenal and that he thought it was a shame that I no longer wanted to play. He encouraged me to come to practice to at least check things out. If I still had no desire to play after doing that, then he would leave me alone. I agreed to his condition because I was sure that attending one practice wouldn't change my mind.

As a kid I used to always look forward to practice. I used to love spending my evenings playing the beautiful game and feeling as if I was doing something that I was really good at. But now, at sixteen, I didn't feel the same love toward the sport and my expectation was that I would practice with this no-name team on that Wednesday night, and then I would walk away from football forever. If I were a betting man, that's the outcome I would have put my money on.

I still get goose bumps now. If I close my eyes I can still feel the ball caressing my foot. The feeling was magical. Over a year had passed since I had last touched a ball, but here I was touching it, passing it, shooting it, and remembering why I had fallen in love with this game in the first place. I was running around with more enthusiasm than I had felt in a long time and I couldn't remember the last time I had been this happy.

With every touch of the ball my happiness grew. I ran like never before, I shot the ball with passion, and I bonded with the seven other kids who were there that night through our mutual affection for this sport. On that cool August evening I reconnected with the one thing that I had always loved. There were no fans in the stands, in fact we didn't even have stands, we were just in a park. There were no television cameras, no media, no money, and no agents. This was football at its core, the sport without the business side. It was raw, just a few teenagers playing in the middle of a park on a Wednesday evening; I loved it.

Up until this day some of my best football memories are the ones that I made when I was ten years old and playing on the concrete in front of my house with the other neighborhood kids. The fun, the enjoyment, the fight, the passion, the will to win, the competition—it was intense. I can assure you that although we had no audience we played as though it was the World Cup Final and millions around the world were watching us. This is what I have always loved about football—the passion it produces in people—and as I practiced with Oscar and this new team that night I began to feel some emotions I had not felt in a very long time. "I've missed this," I said to myself. "I've really, really missed this." I felt no apprehension in regard to my knee. I felt completely free during that whole practice session.

After about two hours of non-stop play, Abbey called the session to a close, but I was already ready to go again. I was physically tired, but my spirit felt rejuvenated. This session had given me life. I kept on asking everyone when the next session would be. I just wanted to get back out there and play with the ball again. After falling out of love with the sport once Arsenal had released me, and then completely running away from it after my moped accident, I was now back where I felt I belonged—on the pitch, doing the thing that I still clearly most loved to do.

That one Wednesday practice session turned into a two-and-a-half-year period of my life where I played with this team. At first I played just to get my fitness back for the sake of getting it back, but then, a few months after I had started playing for this team, I decided that I would once again try and live the dream I had always aspired to live, and so I began to use this team as a springboard into professional football.

We were practicing twice a week at that point, and with each passing week I fell more and more in love with the game again. My passion and hunger were slowly being rekindled, and it was obvious to me, and to everyone else on the team, that this was what I wanted to do with the rest of my life. I wanted to play professionally.

With my encouragement, Abbey began inviting scouts from professional teams to watch me play. In the two and a half years I was with this team—we still had no official name, so I referred to it as "Abbey's

Team"—I played in tournaments in the U.S. and in Italy, and I had unsuccessful tryouts with teams from The Netherlands, Spain, and England. I
got so used to being rejected by teams and hearing the word "no" that it
no longer bothered me when a team turned me down. I just simply went
on to the next one. Abbey was instrumental in getting me these tryouts
because he emailed video footage of every one of the games that I played,
as well as my football CV—which was a list of the teams I'd played on
and my accomplishments while playing with them, to hundreds of teams
worldwide. We hardly ever got a response from these teams, and when
we did it was usually to say, "Thanks, but no thanks."

Only a handful of teams, from the hundreds, agreed to bring me
in on trial, and that was only because I had offered to pay my own
travel and lodging expenses. I had very little money in those days, and
so Abbey either paid most of the costs for me or I found a way to raise
money before a trip.

I stayed in the cheapest hotels, I cooked my own food to keep
costs down, and whenever it was possible I traveled across Europe by
train rather than plane, because that was a lot cheaper. If a team agreed
to bring me in, I didn't care where in the world they were located, I
would find a way to get there. I had one single pair of boots that I wore
in every game for two and a half years. I washed them in a bathtub
every few weeks to keep them fresh, and I carried them around in a
plastic bag as I boarded the planes and trains to my next trial.

I became close with Abbey during this period because he believed
in me and pushed me. After my first two weeks of training with his
team we had a conversation:

"Steve, I see a lot of talent in you. But the player I see before me is
not the player that I once saw at Arsenal."

"Ok, so what am I lacking?" I asked, curious to know his thoughts.

Abbey didn't hold back, "You're one step too slow. You need to get
stronger, and you also need to get fitter."

I never took his words as criticism. I knew he was just being honest,
"Okay, can you help me do those things?"

"As long as you're willing to put the work in, I'll help you."

"Yeah, I'm willing."

And so it began. Because I didn't have a job and I wasn't attending
school, I was free to invest most of my time into training with Abbey.
I got my football training in twice a week with the rest of the team,
but on the days when there was no team training scheduled I did my

own personal training with Abbey. Here is what a typical week would look like for me in that two-and-a-half-year period that I played with Abbey's team:

Monday – Send out video footage to pro teams. Team practice.
Tuesday – One-on-one speed training with Abbey. Weight training.
Wednesday – Team practice.
Thursday – Two mile run.
Friday – Hill sprints with Abbey.
Saturday – Game
Sunday – Off Day (Thank God!)

For speed training I used to do two separate things. The first thing I did was called parachute-sprints. Abbey would tie a parachute around my waist and I would sprint ten yards forward, turn, and then sprint back to the start line. I would then sprint twenty yards forward and back. And then I would do the same for thing thirty, forty, and fifty yards.

When you sprint with a parachute around your waist, at first it just lies on the ground, but as you take off and pick up speed it lifts off into the air and provides great resistance for you to run against. Those sprints were very challenging, but they were nothing compared to the second type of speed training I did—hill sprints.

There was a hill not too far from Abbey's house called Hammer's Hill. It was very steep and about half a mile long. Once a week, late in the evening, Abbey would take me to the hill and I would do eight sprints at the steepest part of the hill before I could go home. The sprints were anywhere from fifty to one hundred yards in length. It was a brutal workout but one that I think helped me to not only regain my speed but also improve it.

My conditioning was either a two-mile run or interval training where I alternated between walking, jogging, and sprinting. Neither of those were fun either. I hate distance running, but I knew it was important for me to build a base fitness level because all of the players at the teams I was going to try out with would be fitter than me. In the gym, I did weights but I never lifted any heavy weights. I'm a skinny guy and I have always been this way. I don't like doing heavy weight-lifting. Even in my professional career I rarely did heavy weightlifting. I normally stuck to doing lots of reps at a lighter weight. This allowed me to build strength while also maintaining my agility and quickness, two very important parts of my game. Looking back, those workouts took a lot out of me both mentally and physically, but I kept doing them because I was seeing results.

My performance on the pitch began to improve, and I began to feel more confident that I was capable of earning a professional contract. After every unsuccessful trial I simply came back to London and worked harder with Abbey. I feel that in life we have to experience failure before we can become successful. Long before I was playing professionally for the Seattle Sounders and the Portland Timbers, in front of forty thousand fans, I was failing all over the place as I tried to earn my contract.

WIGAN ATHLETIC

At the time (September 2004), Wigan Athletic were playing in the English Championship, which is one level below the world famous English Premier League. Abbey had developed a relationship with the Director of the Wigan Youth Academy, and because of that they asked him to send four or five of his best players for a tryout. I was in that group, and so was Oscar. We took the National Express (a bus service in the U.K. like Greyhound in the U.S.) from London to Manchester, where the Youth Academy Director, John Williams, picked us up. He drove us from Manchester to Wigan, which was about a thirty-minute drive, and we spent the first night at his house before he placed us in a hotel for the remainder of our stay.

I remember arriving in Manchester and seeing Old Trafford, one of the most famous football stadiums in the world and home to one of the biggest football teams in the world, Manchester United. Old Trafford is nicknamed The Theatre of Dreams, and as John Williams's car drove by it I felt as though my own dream was finally going to come to fruition at Wigan. I couldn't have been more wrong.

After just four days of training they informed me that they wouldn't be signing me because they didn't see a future for me at the club. Only Oscar had his tryout extended. The rest of us were to leave for London the next day. Being the teenagers that we were, we decided to go out in style. We were staying at a hotel called the Bellington Hotel, and on their dinner menu they had a $120 item called the Bellington Combo.

The Combo was a mixture of chicken, beef, pork, shrimp, and duck dishes rolled into one big meal that was to be shared among three people at the very least. There were three of us who had been told we wouldn't be signing with Wigan and we ordered one Combo each. We also ordered several bottles of wine and champagne (who celebrates getting turned down by a team?), and a bunch of desserts.

I didn't drink the wine or champagne but I enjoyed the dessert and the chicken-beef-pork-duck-shrimp dish; up until this day it's still one of the best dinners that I've ever had. Later that night we ordered several movies and a lot of room service; we stayed up all night enjoying ourselves. But here's the real kicker: Wigan Athletic were the ones who had to pay for all of this because we were on their tab. When they brought us up to try out and had agreed to pay for our hotel rooms and our meals they obviously never expected us to abuse that courtesy in the way that we did. Our grand total for that one night was $1,500! Add to that the other three nights and our bill was about $3,000 by the time we checked out of the hotel.

We had already boarded the National Express and were on our way back to London before word got back to John Williams from the hotel about what we had done. His relationship with Abbey ended soon after that.

AZ ALKMAAR

I tried out with AZ Alkmaar, one of the great Dutch teams, in January of 2006. I was supposed to be there for seven days but I ended up leaving after only three. Abbey accompanied me on the trip and we stayed at a Best Western Hotel about twenty minutes from their practice facility. During my first training session every single player took part in a skills challenge. I looked around and they were all doing an amazing job.

There was one guy who particularly impressed because of the ease with which he was completing this challenge. When the coach blew the whistle to end the skills challenge he announced that the next activity would be shooting practice. He told the goalies to get their gloves and get in the goal. I watched in complete astonishment as the guy who had impressed me the most dropped his ball, picked up his gloves, and went in the goal. He was the goalie!

After seeing what the goalie could do with his feet, I could only imagine what the rest of the players would be capable of doing. I knew I wasn't at the level required to play for this team quite yet and so I cut my trip short.

FC TOP OSS

Top Oss was also a Dutch team, although they were one league below AZ Alkmaar, and their goalies were nowhere near as good with their feet as the AZ Alkmaar goalies. I went to Top Oss immediately after I left AZ Alkmaar because I felt that it would be less challenging than what I had experienced at AZ Alkmaar, and it was. I played well during my weeklong trial and they really wanted to sign me but the only problem was that they didn't have any money. They weren't able to complete my signing because they wouldn't have been able to pay me. They were a smaller club with a tight budget, and even though I was disappointed I had no choice but to move on.

QUEENS PARK RANGERS

Queens Park Rangers, who are now playing in the English Premier League, invited me to train with them in the summer of 2005. It wasn't specified how long they wanted me to train with them, but I assumed I would be there for at least a few days so they would have enough time to get a proper feel for me. How wrong I was! After just one forty-five-minute training session, in which we did very little actual playing (we warmed up, did a passing drill, and then a shooting drill, never actually doing anything resembling a game setting), the coach told me to not bother returning the next day.

Abbey asked him why he didn't want me to return for a second day, and his response was that my running style showed that I wasn't supposed to be a footballer. I left the room as Abbey argued with him.

REAL VALLADOLID

My favorite player of all time is the Brazilian Ronaldinho. Between 2003 and 2006 he was at the peak of his powers while playing for the

Spanish team Barcelona. I admired him and I loved watching Spanish football. I felt that the style of play in Spain suited me better than what I was used to in England, so I began reaching out to Spanish teams. The only one to respond was Real Valladolid. (Don't worry, I couldn't pronounce their name either when I first read it.)

They invited me to train with them for a week and I had a great time. I felt that Spain was a tremendous country to live in because of the weather, the culture, and the style of football. Unfortunately, although I did okay during training, they didn't think that I had shown that I was good enough to play for them.

All of these failures were actually what made me succeed in the end because I kept learning from them. Every time I was in a professional environment I would study the players in my position to see what they did and didn't do, and then I would try to implement their habits into my own game, and I always added my own twist, of course. But I can't lie and say that I wasn't a little disheartened after the multiple failed attempts at getting a contract.

I had been working day and night with Abbey, I was as fit as I had ever been, and I was playing the best football of my life at that point; so it was disappointing to be turned away everywhere I went. Nevertheless, something inside me wouldn't allow me to quit. I was really hungry again, hungrier than ever. I felt that I just had to get my foot in the door, any door, and then I knew I would be successful after that. Since the professional teams didn't seem keen on me, Abbey proposed another idea for me to consider.

"Maybe you should go and play college soccer in America and then get drafted into MLS?"

I had no idea what he was talking about. "College what?"

"College soccer."

"What's that?"

"It's where professional teams in America get their players. You attend classes but you also get to play at a high level in great facilities. You can play there, develop your game, and then an MLS team can draft you when you're ready," Abbey explained.

"MLS?"

"Major League Soccer."

I'd heard of it, "Oh, Freddy Adu's league?"

"Yeah, that one," Abbey confirmed.

"Okay."

"Well, what do you think? I've been inviting some college coaches to our practices but I've never told them about you because you wanted to go pro in Europe. Do you want me to reach out to them and tell them about you?"

"I don't know, man. Going back to school to play? I don't know, Abbey."

Sensing my lack of enthusiasm at the thought of going back to school, Abbey said, "I'll tell you what, tomorrow there is a coach coming to watch Oscar. He's from the University of Akron. He's going to watch us practice and then I can have him talk to you afterward. How does that sound?"

"Yeah, that sounds alright."

"Okay, so just come and practice tomorrow and then you can pick his brain after about anything college soccer related."

"Okay cool."

The next afternoon I did what Abbey had told me to do. I came to practice, I played, and then after the session I sat and talked with the coach from the University of Akron. His name was Ryan Higginbotham.

We met at Oscar's house, and aside from Ryan, Oscar, and me, Oscar's mom and Abbey were also present. We all sat in Oscar's living room as Ryan played us two DVDs. The first was a short DVD about the university's academic programs, and the second was a slightly longer one about their soccer team. We were all impressed by what we saw.

The next fifteen minutes consisted of Ryan answering all of our questions, most of them from Oscar's mom. "How many students attend the school? How many games in a season? Is Akron any good at soccer? Where is Akron? What are the chances of being drafted into MLS? Do I have to pass my classes if I want to keep playing? Are the classes difficult?" After Ryan was done answering all of our questions he turned to us and said, "So, what do you think? Do you guys wanna come to Akron?" I told him that I would think about it. That was my polite way of saying no.

Despite being impressed by Ryan's presentation I still wanted to try out for a few more teams in Europe before I went back to school on a different continent. Oscar, on the other hand, had already made his mind up: he wanted to go to Akron. When I got home that night I had a conversation with my parents about Ryan and Akron. I showed them the same DVDs that he had shown me. They were both very impressed, primarily with the educational aspect of this deal, and they encouraged me to pursue the opportunity if that was what I wanted to do. As I went to sleep that night I still wasn't entirely sure if going to college in the U.S. was what I wanted to do. I was still dreaming of playing in Europe.

Over the next couple of weeks an influx of coaches from different American colleges came to London to watch me play for Abbey's team. The University of Connecticut, the University of Dayton, the University of North Carolina at Chapel Hill, Florida International University, and Creighton were just some of the colleges whose coaches I met and had conversations with about playing college soccer.

The more and more I talked to these coaches the more and more I was leaning toward going to the U.S. on a soccer scholarship. I was realizing that it hadn't worked out for me in Europe and that going to the U.S. might be my last chance to become a pro. If I went to America I was going to get a chance to continue to play soccer while working toward my degree, and if I didn't make it as a pro I would at least have my education.

That line of thinking led me to decide that I was done with trying in Europe, and that it was now time to go across the Atlantic and play college soccer. I told my parents about my decision, and then I spoke to Abbey and told him as well. Once the decision of going to America was made, the only question that remained was which college I would go to. The decision was actually a lot easier than you might think.

Although all of the coaches had sold their own programs really well and given me some amazing presentations, it was Ryan from Akron who stood out most to me. After Ryan had returned to the U.S. we had stayed in touch by email and the occasional phone call. He had introduced me to the head coach at Akron, Caleb Porter, who had also done a good job of reaching out to me. I didn't have those phone and email follow-up conversations with any of the other coaches, so I chose Akron based on how personable their coaches had been. They were the only ones who called me just to see how I was doing and to get updates on my family.

I now realize that they may not have really cared about my family or about how I was doing and were just playing the recruiting game better than the others, but at the time it made a huge impression on me and I decided to go with them.

It was in late June or July of 2006 that I finally made the decision to attend Akron. All that was left for me to do was take the SATs so that I could be admitted into the university. Because of my poor grades at secondary school I needed to score a pretty high SAT score to be accepted into the University of Akron. I was relaxed and confident about the English part of the test; it was the math side that had me worried.

I have never been good at math, and if my past performances on math exams were anything to go by I would need to do some serious studying if I was to stand a chance of passing the math portion of the SAT exam. I had about two months to study for the SATs, and I spent almost every waking hour studying math. I was scheduled to take my SATs in September 2006, and if all went well I would head to Akron, a place I had never even heard of before meeting Ryan, in January 2007.

Things were finally starting to look up for me. I had undergone a massive change in my approach to football since I had met Abbey, and between his training methods and my own renewed dedication I had managed to give myself a chance of becoming a pro in the United States. There was still a lot of work to do before I could ever sign a professional contract, but at least I had put myself in a good position and given myself a good chance.

Away from football my life had also undergone some major changes. Between the time I first went to play for Abbey's team (August 2004) and the time I stepped foot on the Akron campus for the very first time (January 2007) there were three major life-changing events that took place off the field. These events shaped me in ways that I will never fully understand. All three events played a part in making me the person I am today. Let me tell you about them.

EVENT ONE – AUGUST 2004

In August 2004 Arnold died. He was murdered in Tottenham. Arnold was one of the most popular people in North London; everyone loved him. He was a great football player and someone that everyone enjoyed being around. The first time I ever met him I was about twelve and he was about sixteen. He and I were both in a large group of friends who were playing football in the park. I remember being so impressed by how good Arnold was; he was doing things with the ball that I had never seen anyone else do at that point in my life, and I wanted to learn from him. My older brother and I became friends with him and his brother on that day. At the time of his death he was only twenty years old.

His death shook our whole community. I didn't realize how popular he was until I attended his funeral. There were hundreds of people there and they were from all walks of life—black, white, old, young, male, female, rich, and poor—every type of person came to celebrate Arnold's life at his funeral. There were kids from rival gangs, who under any other circumstances would have been starting a fight the second they saw each other, that were walking side by side mourning and comforting one another.

A lot of our parents also came to the funeral, as did many community leaders. Judging by the turnout at his funeral, anyone could see that he was loved by a lot of people. After the viewing at the church we all marched several miles from the church to the burial site, all of us dressed in black and exchanging stories and memories about him.

I had never experienced the loss of someone so young and close to me before, and from the moment it happened I had a very hard time accepting that it was true. I think another reason why his death hit me especially hard was that he had a story that was very similar to mine. He had grown up in London, but like me he was originally from the Congo, and he was also a gifted footballer with the potential to play at a professional level. I think about him every single day, and no matter how much time passes (as I write these words the ten-year anniversary of his death has just passed) he is never far from my thoughts.

I remember playing a game against the Colorado Rapids in August of 2010 while I was still playing with the Seattle Sounders. The game fell on a date close to the sixth anniversary of his death and I decided to write a message to him on a piece of paper that I taped on my left and right wrists. I scored two goals in that game and as I celebrated one of my goals I looked up to the sky and pointed my wrists toward the heavens as a tribute to him. I wanted him to see the message. I have scored far better goals in my career, but none have been as meaningful as the two that I scored on that day because those goals were not for me, they were for Arnold. His death put the brevity of life into perspective for me. Up until that point I was under the impression that the only people that died were old people, or those with terminal illnesses. To see someone who wasn't much older than me, someone who was in perfectly good health, have his life cut short, it made a big impression on me and it scared me in some ways.

EVENT TWO – APRIL 2005

On a warm night in April 2005 I was out with some friends at a mini-carnival that took place in one of the parks in North London. It was a Friday night and I was with about eight of my friends. Even though the carnival wasn't particularly memorable, this is a night that I will remember for the rest of my life because of what took place right after the carnival had finished.

We were standing outside of a McDonald's restaurant at about ten o'clock and although it was late the streets were still busy and a lot of people were out enjoying themselves at the various pubs and bars. Some people had come from the carnival, and others were out simply because it was a Friday night. I remember that we weren't the only group of teenagers that was standing outside the McDonald's; there were about six or seven other large groups of boys right next to our group. Naturally, there were also a lot of girls around too, because we always went wherever the girls were.

Nothing out of the ordinary was taking place; there was a lot of laughter, animated conversations, and loud music playing from a few car stereos. Some people were eating, others were smoking, and some of us were just standing there making jokes and being teenagers. There was nothing to suggest that this night was about to explode into senseless violence that almost claimed two lives.

This scene remained the same until almost without warning an altercation broke out between one of my friends and another kid. It all began because of the way my friend had looked at the other guy. That might sound crazy to you, but where I came from there was definitely a right way and a wrong way to look at someone. There was a lot of shouting and commotion as a crowd began to gather around the two of them. I was standing about fifty feet away from where this had all taken place when I saw the other kid swing a punch at my friend. After that swing and miss all hell broke loose.

A full-fledged brawl began taking place right there on the streets as the two guys—my friend and the other kid—were joined by their groups of friends. It was our group against their group. The fight couldn't have lasted more than twenty seconds, but at the time, in the midst of battle, it seemed to go on for an eternity. There were about fourteen teenagers throwing fists, swinging legs, and grabbing each other as the two groups went toe to toe over the way one boy had looked at another boy.

There is no way of knowing what would have happened or how much worse it would have gotten if the police hadn't shown up. As we were fighting the sound of sirens and screeching tires suddenly pierced the evening sky. I heard the police way before I saw them. One minute we were fighting, and the next a police car had mounted the curb.

One of the police cars came to a stop within inches of where we were fighting. Someone from the crowd yelled out, "It's the feds. Run!" We didn't need to be told twice. We stopped fighting and ran for it. We all took off in different directions, even the bystanders who weren't involved in the fight.

After a fight like that, regardless of whether or not you had been fighting, the last thing you wanted to do was get cornered by the police. It was much easier to run than to convince the police that you knew nothing about the fight. I ran off in the same direction as one of my good friends, Samir. I had known Samir for a few years, and at the time of the fight we were both playing for Abbey's team.

At first our friendship was based on football, but of late we had been getting drawn more and more into the street life. We had been spending a lot of time together and this wasn't the first time we had gotten into a fight with some strangers. This particular fight, though, had been the worst of them. As we ran down some back streets away from the streetlights and the police, a nasty memory came to my mind. I remembered during the fight seeing one of the other boys pull out a knife before stabbing one of my friends. I wasn't sure exactly which friend he had stabbed but I was quite certain that I had seen a shiny blade go into someone's back. Things had happened so fast during the fight that I had almost forgotten about it, but it was now vividly replaying itself in my mind as I ran from the police.

Could Samir have been that friend, the one who was stabbed? I wasn't sure. There was only one way to find out. As we kept running, I asked Samir a question that made him stop dead in his tracks.

"Samir, did you get stabbed?"

My question had confused him. "Stabbed? No way. I never got stabbed, did I?"

"I think you did."

Adamantly, he replied, "No man, I don't think so,"

"Bro, please just check to be sure. I think you got stabbed, man." I was convinced he was the one.

"Okay, let's check," he reluctantly agreed.

I went and stood behind him, and began lifting his shirt. The world seemed to slow down, and the magnitude of what I was about to potentially find out dawned on me. Growing up where I did I had heard of people who had been stabbed, but I had never seen it happen with my own eyes. I felt nervous and tense as I prayed for Samir to not be the friend that had been stabbed. I tried to convince myself that I had imagined it all, but there are some things you just can't deny. I knew that I had seen a shiny blade go into someone's back. I positioned myself directly behind Samir and lifted up his shirt. Blood everywhere, all over his back. "Yes, see, I told you they stabbed you."

Once I said that, the look on his face was one of shock. His eyes widened and he bent over to catch his breath. But before we could allow this new revelation to sink in we had to start running again because we heard the police sirens getting closer.

Samir had already run quite a distance from the fight scene, but this time as he tried to get going again he began stumbling and gasping for air. He was getting weaker, so he leaned on me for support. My mind was racing and my heart was pumping. We were drenched in sweat, exhausted, and struggling to compose ourselves. We knew that he couldn't keep running much longer, so we decided to stop in the front yard of a nearby house. Samir leaned against the gate that led to the yard and I immediately made some phone calls to the rest of our friends to see where they were, and to let them know what had happened. It didn't take long for them to find us.

Once we were all reunited we discovered that from our group of eight, two had been stabbed. Samir hadn't been the only one. Fear and panic set in. *Were they going to die? How deep were the wounds? Had any of us stabbed any of them?*

In the end, Samir lived. He had a life-saving emergency surgery later that night and was able to make a full recovery in the weeks that followed, but this incident had shaken me to my core, and the fragility of life was once again at the forefront of my mind. At the time I was really close to Samir, and to see him on the brink of death was a big wake-up call for me. I knew that I couldn't keep living that lifestyle.

On June 11, 2005, a Saturday night, I was in Tottenham hanging out with some friends. We had spent the entire day playing video games and eating fried chicken. This had become a bit of a routine for me, because when I wasn't playing football with Abbey or trying out for a team somewhere in Europe I spent all of my free time with the same group of friends in Tottenham. These friends were all at least two or three years older than me, and even though most of them sold and used drugs I was always around them because they looked after me like a younger brother. We could easily spend eight hours sitting in one of their living rooms, playing FIFA, eating chicken, drinking alcohol, and smoking weed and cigarettes.

The days would go by in a blur because once we got together we shut out the outside world. At times I felt like I had only been with them for an hour or two, but when I got up to leave it would turn out that several hours had actually passed. I never drank or smoked, but every time I left their presence I stunk of weed and cigarettes because of how much they all smoked around me. Although there was peer pressure to smoke and drink, I was able to resist it because when I was playing for Arsenal my coaches told me to avoid smoking and drinking because it would affect my performances. They said that an athlete had to take care of his or her body. I've never strayed from that advice.

As I hung out with them there would be times when I would feel as if I was wasting my life away. Not only were they bad role models for me to have but they also weren't encouraging me to want to do something positive with my life. Around them I kind of just existed without ever doing much. Whenever I got home from spending my day with them I was always left with a nagging feeling that I had just thrown my day away. Deep down I felt that there had to be ways in which I could make far better use of my time.

When I got home on June 11 after a day of FIFA and fried chicken one of my brothers had a message for me: "Call Mr. Goodison. He called here earlier looking for you." It had been months since I'd last spoken to Mr. Goodison, but the sheer mention of his name brought back some good memories for me. I looked at my watch—eleven—it was late, so I decided to wait until the next day to call him. But then my brother came back in my room and told me that Mr. Goodison had also said that I should call him that same night because it was urgent.

"Hello?"

Sir, it's me. It's Steve.

"Oh, Steve, how are you?" He sounded genuinely happy to hear from me.

"I'm good. Sorry if I'm calling too late."

"No problem at all, it's never too late. How are things?"

I decided to be vague and brief. "They're okay. I'm back playing football again, so that's good. Other things in my life aren't as good as they could be, but that's life."

He asked, "Where are you playing?"

"Just on an amateur team. But I've gotten a few trials to some pro teams, they just haven't worked out yet. But I'll keep trying. How are things with you?" I wanted to get the attention away from me and onto him. I didn't want him to ask me if I had been applying the things he had taught me, because I hadn't.

"I'm good, and the family is good."

"That's good to hear, sir."

"Okay, well I won't keep you long, so I'll cut to the chase. Tomorrow morning I want you to come to a leadership seminar with me."

Genuinely confused, I replied, "A leadership what?"

Mr. Goodison explained. "A seminar. It's kind of like . . . it's an event where everyone comes together to hear a speaker talk about leadership."

"A speaker?"

"Yes, a speaker. It'll be good for you. It's been going on for a few days and tomorrow is the last day. I don't want you to miss it. The speaker is very good."

"Hmm, well I don't know about that sir. A seminar? What is he speaking about?"

"Leadership."

Just to confirm I had been hearing him correctly, I said, "A leadership seminar?"

"Yes. You will enjoy it. Everyone I have invited so far has loved it and you will be no different. I can pick you up from your house at nine o'clock tomorrow."

"Nine a.m.? But it's Sunday tomorrow, that's when I usually sleep in," I protested.

"Well, it starts at ten, and it's in East London, so I need to get you at nine."

Sensing that he wouldn't take no for an answer, I said, "I guess that's fine."

"Great. I'll call you when I'm outside. Have a good rest of the night, Steve."

"Thanks, you too, sir."

The next morning, I woke up, took my phone off silent mode, and saw that I had five missed calls. I checked the time—9:05. Crap! He's here. I've overslept. I thought about going back to sleep and then calling Mr. Goodison later that evening to tell him that I had woken up with a massive headache, which is why I never answered his calls or came to the seminar, but my conscience got the better of me and I sent him a text: "Will be out in a bit." I then proceeded to have the fastest shower in human history. I was literally in and out in less than two minutes. I got dressed in five minutes, and then I ran into the kitchen to drink some orange juice before I headed out to his car.

I walked up to the driver's side to greet Mr. Goodison. We shook hands, I apologized for being late, and then I got in on the passenger's side. We didn't talk much on the thirty-minute drive to East London. Mr. Goodison's music played softly in the background, and aside from one or two questions about my family and what I had been up to since leaving school the music played uninterrupted for the duration of our drive. I had no idea what to expect from a leadership seminar because I had never been to or heard of one before. I was just really hoping that whatever a leadership seminar was it didn't last too long.

As we pulled up to the venue I couldn't help but notice that the building looked like an old, abandoned warehouse. If this is where they hold leadership seminars, then it's no wonder that I have never heard of one. This building looks terrible! Sensing my disapproval of the building, Mr. Goodison quickly assured me that the inside of the building was much easier on the eyes than the outside. His words proved to be true, because from the moment we stepped inside I was impressed by the interior design of the building. The carpets were clean, the art on the wall was eye-catching, and the auditorium was filled with about two thousand people. *I guess a leadership seminar can't be all that bad if two thousand people are prepared to waste their Sunday mornings by coming here!*

We made our way to the back of the auditorium. Mr. Goodison

had spotted a couple of empty seats and he hurried toward them before someone could beat us there. Once we were seated we made some small talk with the people sitting next to us, and then the event finally got under way. The event host welcomed everyone in attendance, told us a bit about the event for a few minutes, let us know how we could buy DVDs of the seminar online, and then he introduced the speaker. Mr. Goodison nudged me gently and said, "Get ready, this brother is the real deal."

As the speaker began to talk I placed my head into my hands and leaned forward so that my forehead was resting on the chair in front of me. I wanted to sleep my way through this talk; I was hoping he would be done by the time I woke up.

"My name is Dr. Myles Munroe, I am from Nassau, Bahamas, and today, I want to talk to you about leadership. When we hear or think of the word leadership, we tend to think that it is something that is reserved for a select few; a special few. We think that leadership is for the rich and famous, or the charismatic people around us. We assume that only a few people will ever become leaders. But I want to tell you that this is simply not true. I flew all the way to London from the Bahamas to tell you that this is not what leadership is about. Leadership is not for a select few; it's for everyone. It's for the person leading a Fortune 500 Company, but it's also for the housewife. Leadership is for the president of a country, but it is also for the person sitting in your chair."

I sat up when he said that part about the chair. *There's a leader in my chair? What is this guy talking about? I'm in my chair! There's no leader here; it's just me.* Myles Munroe continued to speak:

"Everyone in this room was born to be a leader, no question about it. You have amazing leadership potential inside of you but it has been buried under your experiences, your fears, your mistakes, and your insecurities. Let me tell you how we are all born to be leaders. We are all born with an amazing gift that we must serve to the world. Every human is born with a gift. Some of you are gifted painters, some of you are gifted musicians, some of you have a gift in politics, and some of you are gifted athletes (Mr. Goodison nudged me when he said that). There are some people in this room who were born to be teachers (I nudged him back), while some of you were born to be authors. There are gifted administrators, and poets, and electricians, and architects, all in this room. You see, whatever you were born to be, when you decide to become it, you will become a leader. When you decide to become who you were born to be you will become so good at what you do that people will begin to follow you; that's how you become a leader."

The room was completely silent as all two thousand of us hung on every word that was coming out of Myles Munroe's mouth:

"You don't become a leader through manipulating people or by seeking to become powerful; you become a leader by serving your gift; by serving the thing that you do well, to your community, and then to the world. All the great leaders in history were simply those who found something that they could serve the world; they were servants. They never sought to make the people follow them; but the people did follow them. And they followed them willfully because the people wanted what they were serving. If you want to be a leader, don't seek power and don't seek a title; seek to be of service and people will follow you."

I looked around the room. People were scribbling furiously in their notepads (this was before the days of iPads and iPhones; people actually wrote things down with their pens—imagine that!).

"The greatest leaders in history were not made in classrooms. They were made the day that they decided they would offer something to the world. What is your gift? I'm talking to everyone in this room. What gift can you serve the world before you die? Don't rob us of your awesome gift, and don't waste it. Serve your gift. If you're a teacher, then teach. If your passion lies in art, then serve that artistic gift to the rest of us. But whatever you do, do something. Doing nothing is no longer an option. I flew from the Bahamas to tell you that every human is a leader. Leadership is for all humans, not for a select group of special people. If you want to be a leader, don't try to make people follow you, simply serve them your gift. That is what makes you a leader; a servant leader."

You could have heard a pin drop in that room. I had never seen anyone be so brilliant with words before. I didn't know anyone who could articulate anything so well and I had never seen anyone control an entire room with their mouth. He had us spellbound. At times it felt as if it was just him and me in the room, because every word he spoke resonated with the core of my being.

"Some of you had dreams that you have given up on. Pick them up again, go after them, achieve them, and then inspire other people to do the same. You were born to be a leader and you need to believe that. You're the only version of you that there will ever be. After you, there won't be another, so make sure you are the best version of you. Go out and be a leader!"

As he left the stage after his presentation I was left in a daze. I had so many thoughts rushing through my mind but I didn't even know how to begin processing what I had just heard. I looked at Mr. Goodison and he just smiled back at me as if to say, *I told you he was good.* I sat there for a few minutes trying to make sense of what I had just heard and why it was making me feel this way. I felt really good inside, better than I had ever felt before. I felt inspired, as if I could go out and conquer the world and achieve all of my dreams. *How could anyone's words have such a powerful and positive impact on me?* I didn't know it in that very moment but Myles Munroe had just changed the entire course of my life.

Once the meeting was over I was told that Myles Munroe had just released a brand new book, The Spirit of Leadership, and that he was giving away free, signed copies to anyone in attendance who had just heard him speak for the first time ever. As soon as I heard about this offer I rushed over to the area where the giveaway was going to take place. I was the first person to make it over there.

A long line quickly formed behind me. We stood in line for about five minutes before Myles Munroe emerged from a side door with his wife and his daughter right behind him. As I watched him walk over to the autograph table I kept replaying his words in my mind. "The person in your chair was born to be a leader." "Leaders don't seek power or titles; they seek to serve. Serve your gift, and people will follow you willingly."

As he sat down I was only about ten feet away from him, the closest I had been to him all day, and I could feel the positive energy emanating from him; it was infectious. He looked up and gave me a big smile as he waved me over to him. My heart skipped a couple of beats. I usually don't get nervous around people but there was just something different about this man; he was unlike any man I had ever met before. I didn't know exactly what it was that made him so different. I just knew that he was.

I walked right up to the table. He smiled at me and extended his hand. I reached out and we shook hands. I looked right at him, right into his eyes, and I saw what I could only describe as peace. I don't know how else to describe what it is that I saw other than to say that when I looked into Myles Munroe's eyes I felt a sense of peace staring back at me. *This man is at peace,* I thought to myself. *I want to be at peace too.*

I was probably at the table getting my book signed for no more than fifteen seconds, but it felt like an eternity; everything seemed to happen in slow motion. While he was signing my book I thought of my life as it was at that moment—no sense of purpose, chaos, drug dealers, drug fiends, violence, stabbings, murders—my life was a shambles. It was a complete and utter mess. I couldn't help but think of the peace I had felt coming from Myles Munroe as we shook hands and I stared into his eyes. I wanted that same peace more than anything in the world. He smiled at me again as he handed me my autographed copy of his book. His wife and daughter also smiled at me as I turned to leave so that those next in line could get their books signed. I walked up to Mr. Goodison and as we began to head for the exit I stopped, turned, took one last look at Myles Munroe, and said to myself, "I want whatever that man has."

Those three events—the death of Arnold, the stabbing of Samir, and hearing Myles Munroe talk about leadership—all affected me in deep but different ways. Arnold's death made me realize how fragile life can be, while Samir's stabbing made me reevaluate the life I was living and the situations I was getting myself into. But it was the third event that made the biggest impression on me.

Hearing Myles Munroe talk about leadership was the one moment, above all others, that transformed me from the person I was into the person that I eventually became. He reached me in a way that nothing ever had before, and he was able to bypass any barriers that I had built up to keep people out in the past.

After that day, June 12, 2005, I went home and asked my parents for money so that I could buy all of his other books and DVDs. He came back to London to speak at a few different events later that year and I was always the first one in the building, sitting in the front row. I stopped hanging out with those friends who were leading me astray, and I began spending all of my spare time reading and studying. I read all of Myles Munroe's books, and I read a lot of autobiographies. I studied and read books on leadership, success, and business. I remember also reading some good books on philosophy, religion, spirituality, politics, relationships, psychology, and sports during that time. Any book that contained good ideas and insights, I read. I spent hours reading the Bible, especially the book of Proverbs because I was drawn to the simple wisdom and leadership advice I found in there.

The way I saw it, I had spent the first seventeen years of my life living at a level well below what I was capable of, and now that Myles Munroe, and Mr. Goodison before him, had lit a fuse under me I was determined to spend the next seventeen years making up for lost time by feeding my mind with all the positive books it could handle. Looking back, I feel as though the best education I ever received was from all of those hours I spent reading on my bedroom floor. The tuition was cheap because I bought most of my books from the used section of Amazon for as low one or two dollars sometimes. I spent at least a year doing nothing but reading, studying, and training with Abbey.

I wouldn't trade what those books taught me for anything in the world, they're the best investment I have ever made, and they equipped me with everything I would need to succeed when I left London and headed to America to pursue my dream.

As the time for me to head to Akron drew closer I wrote down my life goals on a piece of paper. Some of them were:

- Become a professional footballer.
- Start an organization that will allow me to give back.
- Read four books a month; never stop learning.
- Host leadership seminars to help people discover their own gifts.

I kept my written goals with me at all times. There were about ten goals in total. I never wanted to live another day without working toward my goals, so I made copies of them and hung them up on my bedroom walls once I got to Akron. Some of my college friends made fun of me for hanging pieces of paper with written goals on them all over my bedroom wall, but for me they were a source of inspiration and a daily reminder of where I was ultimately headed.

I arrived in Akron, Ohio on January 13 2007, and although I spent only two years there they remain two of the best years of my life. One day, once I have accomplished a lot more in my life, I hope to be able to write a full autobiography that can detail a lot of the unique experiences I had at Akron. Aside from the numerous awards I won while playing at the school—Soccer America Player of the Year, College Soccer Top Scorer, and of course being the number one overall draft pick in the 2009 Major League Soccer SuperDraft—what I am most proud of from my time there are the friendships I was able to develop.

There's just something about living with, attending class with, and being on a team with the same group of guys that draws you to one another and forms unbreakable bonds. A lot of my really good friends today are people that I met during my brief two-year stay at the University of Akron.

From the moment I arrived on campus, after the initial shock of seeing more snow than I had ever seen in my entire my life and waking up to thirty-degree weather had passed, Akron was everything that Ryan had told me it would be when he had sat down with me in London. I enjoyed going to class, and although I found it challenging at times because I had been out of formal education for three years before going to Akron I still had a really good time learning all the different things that I was taught. I lived in off-campus housing in a house with three of my teammates. They were older than me and made my transition from London to Ohio a lot easier than it perhaps could have been.

On the field, my time at Akron went exceptionally well. After a decent freshman year I exploded in my sophomore year. I scored twenty goals in twenty-three games to lead the nation in scoring, and our team made it to the second round of the NCAA tournament before losing 1-0 in overtime. I was fortunate to play with some really good players who allowed me to be successful while I was at Akron. Most of the guys I played with have gone on to have professional football careers in MLS and abroad. Some of the guys I played with at Akron include:

Anthony Ampaipitakwong (Thailand)
Darlington Nagbe (Portland Timbers)
Michael Nanchoff (Portland Timbers)
Ben Zemanski (Portland Timbers)
Blair Gavin (Chivas Usa, Atlanta Silverbacks FC)
Kofi Sarkodie (Houston Dynamo)
Chris Korb (DC United)
Evan Bush (Montreal Impact)
Teal Bunbury (New England Revolution)

There are many more players who have gone from playing at

Akron into the professional game but those are the ones that I played with. It was during my sophomore year that whispers of interest from MLS and some teams back home began to surface. I arrived at Akron with the dream of becoming a professional footballer, and so, even though I was enjoying my education, when MLS made a contract offer to me in January 2009 it was impossible for me to say no to it. I went to Akron on January 13, 2007, with a clear mission in mind: to play well at Akron, become a professional footballer, and then to use my professional platform to give back, especially to those who are in the kind of situations that I was once in. I had the kids in Tottenham, the ones I had left behind, in mind when I first began to dream of being someone who would help others emerge from troubled pasts into brighter futures.

That's why when I signed my professional contract it wasn't about money or about fame for me, it was about checking one of my goals off of my list, just one small goal that was hopefully going to lead me to bigger and better things.

The process of signing a contract and leaving Akron was a fairly quick one. Once we had lost in the NCAA tournament in late November I had lunch with my head coach at Akron, Caleb Porter, and he asked me directly if I wanted to stay in college for another year or if I wanted to leave and sign a professional contract. I thought about it for a few minutes and without me saying much he could tell that my heart was set on becoming a professional. He told me that he felt I was making the right decision and that the next step was for me to sign with an agent who could represent me in my negotiations with MLS.

I met with quite a few agents and agencies before I decided to sign with the one I felt the best connection with, and that was Wasserman Media Group. More specifically, my contract was going to be negotiated by Richard Motzkin and Leo Cullen, two great agents and great people who I later became good friends with. Within a week of signing, WMG negotiated my first professional contract with MLS and an endorsement deal with Adidas. Just like that I had gone from being an amateur college soccer player to signing with MLS and having an agent as well as an endorsement deal. As I was signing all of those papers it didn't really sink in that I was now a professional footballer; that moment of realization wouldn't come until a couple of weeks after I had signed all the paperwork and contracts. After signing my contract I had a month to spare before the MLS SuperDraft. I flew home for the

Christmas holidays and spent time with my friends and family. I visited Mr. Goodison at his house, and I also spent some time with Abbey, two men who had played key roles in me signing a professional contract.

January 15, 2009, was the day that it first hit me that I had realized my dream and was now a professional footballer. It was the day of the MLS SuperDraft, and as I stood onstage after being selected first overall by the Seattle Sounders, it was then that it sunk in. It was then that I saw the payoff from my years of hard work. The days of running up Hammer's Hill with Abbey and doing parachute-sprints in the park finally seemed worth it.

The draft was exactly two years and two days from the day that I had first arrived in the U.S. at the University of Akron. It was five and a half years since I had crashed that stolen moped, four and a half years since that phone call I received from Oscar inviting me to play for Abbey's team, and three and a half years since I had heard Myles Munroe speak at the leadership seminar. I'd experienced some pretty big moments in my life thus far, and this draft day was another one. I have often kept journals and diaries at different times in my life to express my thoughts about what is happening in my life; here is an entry that I wrote after draft day as I tried to relive the experience.

JANUARY 15 2009

Before the Draft

I woke up at seven o'clock and as I lay on my bed in my hotel room in St. Louis, Missouri, I replied to all the emails I had gotten over the past few days. After that, I take a shower. I shower extra long because I wanna be fresh at the 2009 Major League Soccer SuperDraft. I'm staying at the Westin and I've decided that this is the nicest hotel I have ever stayed in. The spacious rooms, comfortable beds, and room service make this experience even better than it already was. I hopped in the shower and as I let the warm water hit my back, I took a trip down memory lane. I thought of all the years that I spent playing at Arsenal; I thought of the trips, the tournaments, and the opportunities I had to play against the best of the best in youth football. Then I thought about the period following my release from Arsenal, the disillusionment, being sucked into the wrong crowd, losing my passion and dream. I thought about Mr. Goodison and Myles Munroe and all of the things I have learned from each of them. I felt grateful. I spent some time thinking about the way I came back into football with that phone call from Oscar. Playing on Abbey's team was a far cry from what I was used to at Arsenal. With Abbey, we either took public transport or packed five or six players into someone's car to get to games. We had no practice gear; we each wore whatever we wanted to. The games we played were usually in different public parks and the only people in attendance were a few random people who happened to be in the park walking their dogs. Now that I'm about to play professional football, I'm going to be playing in front of a lot more people, thousands even; I can't wait. After leaving the shower, I put my suit on and headed downstairs to meet all of the other players who were also going to be drafted. A shuttle bus took us from the convention center to the hotel.

After

At the draft I sat next to my agents and my college coaches. I didn't really feel any nerves until Don Garber, the MLS commissioner, took the stage and was about to announce the first player to be picked in the draft. Seattle had the first pick and I wanted to go there because I had heard they'd sold nineteen thousand season tickets. They'd also signed Ljungberg and Keller, two players I knew from TV. Alexi Lalas had called my hotel room yesterday and asked me where I wanted to go. I said Seattle. He's doing TV coverage today. I wonder if they mentioned that when they talked about me. I knew that I could end up in any one of the sixteen cities that had MLS teams. I didn't want to play or live in Canada, so that ruled out Toronto FC on my list of preferred destinations. Aside from that, I was just excited to get my professional career started wherever that may be. The ESPN cameras were there, as were several other reporters, media outlets, and publications. When I heard the commissioner say, "With the first pick of the 2009 MLS SuperDraft, the Seattle Sounders select, from the University of Akron . . ." I didn't even wait for the commissioner to say my name, because once I heard him say Akron I knew he was talking about me. Happiness. Yeah, happiness was the overriding emotion flowing through my veins. I was happy that my journey had brought me to this point, happy that I was going to start my career in America, a country I loved living in, and happy that I was going to be playing for the new

MLS team, Seattle. I gave a quick thank you speech, did about a hundred interviews, and then I flew back to Ohio that evening with a stop in Chicago on the way. It was when I laid my head back to sleep on the plane ride that it all sunk in. I was now a professional footballer. Yes, there was still a lot of work ahead, but I wanted to at least acknowledge this accomplishment because it hadn't been easy by any means. I was a professional. I smiled, let out a deep breath, and rocked my head back as I fell asleep filled with excitement at the prospect of the next phase of my journey that awaited me in Seattle.

STEVE

January 15, 2009

Chicago

There you have it. Those were my thoughts on the day that Seattle drafted me. The above journal entry is the best way for me to describe what happened on draft day, because my memory is all over the place when I try to think back to that day. There was just so much going on.

As a side note, at the time when I was deciding whether or not I would sign with MLS or go back to England I had a strong offer from an English team, but I chose to sign with MLS because of a clause in the contract. In my MLS contract there was a clause that said MLS would pay for me to go back and finish school if I ever decided to do so. Having the option to eventually finish my education is what swayed the deal for me at the time.

A lot happened on draft day and in the days that immediately followed—I packed my bags in Ohio and moved to Seattle, Washington. I had to buy a cell phone because I never used one in college, and I had four hundred new Facebook friend requests—but most importantly, I had to get myself ready to start my professional football career.

A love affair with the beautiful game that had begun on a family vacation at Butlins fifteen years ago was about to take me to the Pacific Northwest, where I would play in front of some of the most passionate fans I have ever seen in my life. My time with the Seattle Sounders FC, as I look back on it, turned out to be nothing short of magical.

Just one of many messages
that inspired me to
make a comeback

Photo by Laurie Hodges ©

Celebrating the first of
two goals against the
Colorado Rapids in 2010
with Jeff Parke, Zach
Scott, and James Riley

Photo by Laurie Hodges ©

Photo by Jane Gershovich ©

40,000 fans hold up "11" cards in the eleventh minute of the
first game following my injury. Goosebumps.

A familiar sight at CenturyLink Field between 2009-2011 – Steve Zakuani sprinting down the left wing.

Photo by Laurie Hodges ©

#11

Photo by Jane Gershovich ©

Celebrating an assist to Eddie Johnson in 2013

Photo by Laurie Hodges ©

Celebrating a goal against Toronto FC in 2010. I had the initials of all my siblings written on my wrist and this is me sending them a kiss in celebration.

Signing a young fan's shirt after a home game in 2011.

Photo by Jane Gershovich ©

Unbreakable.

'No caption needed'

Photo by Laurie Hodges ©

Celebrating a goal with
my friends Fredy and
Ossie, two of the best
I ever played with.

Photo by Laurie Hodges ©

Sharing a joke with Sigi. We've always had a brutally honest, but genuine relationship. I'll always be grateful for what he did for me in my career.

Photo by Jane Gershovich ©

We had some great 1v1 battles in training and I am not surprised with where his career is taking him.

Photo by Laurie Hodges ©

Greeting the Sounders faithful in 2014 after announcing my retirement from the game.

Photo by Jane Gershovich ©

Posing with some young soccer players at a tournament I hosted. Rabbit ears all around.

Engaging with fans, young and old, is priceless every time.

A Kodak moment - forgiveness.

Most people are afraid of public speaking. For some odd reason I've always loved it.

Speaking on leadership at my third annual Rising Leaders seminar.

Photo by Jane Gershovich ©

Photo by Jane Gershovich ©

The people responsible for making Kingdom Hope a success thus far. Andrey, Katie, Laurie, and Stephen.

Photo by Leonardo da Costa and Animish Kudalkar ©

The future – Kingdom Hope Football Academy

CHAPTER 7
HEAVEN AND HELL

"Every adversity, every failure, every heartache carries
with it the seed of an equal or greater benefit."

—NAPOLEON HILL

The day began like every other day but it would end like no day ever had. It was a game day, so I slept in later than I normally did on other days. I always used game days as a chance to catch up on all of the sleep I didn't get during the practice week when I had to be up at seven thirty every morning. On game days, especially when the game was in the evening, I could easily sleep in until eleven o'clock or later.

Throughout my career my coaches often told me that being a footballer was the best job in the world, and when I really thought about it, it was hard to disagree with them. How many people can say that they got to do the thing they loved most in front of thousands of people in the stands and many more watching at home for a living? I had so much fun playing football that it felt as if I was being paid to enjoy my favorite hobby. Most of the time my job never really felt like a job at all; I was being paid to have fun. On that Friday morning, as I woke up, unlocked my phone, and checked my email I had no idea that this day was about to become a day that would turn my whole world upside down. The events that would unfold later in the day would lead me to some very dark places, where I had to confront, among other things, the unbearable thought of retirement at twenty-three.

My roommate for road games was Patrick Ianni. Pat and I had become very close during our first two years on the Sounders, and our off-field friendship always made our road trips a more enjoyable experience than they already were. Pat and I had both been with the

Sounders since day one, and even though we were very different in
many ways, he had quickly become one of my best friends. Some of
the ways in which we were different were as follows:

- Pat practiced and played games with the exact same intensity. He
  had no on and off switch, he was one hundred percent go all the
  time. I thought he was crazy. I practiced hard, but I also tried to
  save some energy for the weekend game. I would have had nothing
  left in the tank for Saturday's game if I practiced at a game intensity Monday through Friday.
- Pat was a beast in the weight room. He genuinely loved the gym
  and lifting weights. I have never loved the gym. I couldn't understand how anyone could find lifting weights fun.
- Pat was super into health and nutrition. He took care of his body
  really well. That was an area in which I aspired to be like him. My
  diet wasn't awful, but I ate way more sugar and junk food than
  I should have at the start of my career. I got better as I got older.
- Pat went to bed really early. Sometimes he would be in bed at nine
  and asleep by nine thirty. At nine o'clock I was just finishing my
  dinner! This was an area in which we had to find a middle ground
  on our road trips.
- Pat was a defender; I was an attacker. He viewed the game from
  a defensive standpoint first, whereas as I tended to view it from
  an attacking perspective. This led to a few disagreements during
  practice over whose fault it was when certain plays went badly.

But in spite of those differences what really made our friendship work
were the areas in which we were similar:

- We both genuinely loved the game of football. We expressed it in
  very different ways, but we both loved it with every fiber of our
  being. We spent hours debating different tactics, games, players,
  teams, and different playing styles over the years.
- We led very similar lifestyles off the field. We both read a lot of
  books and had an interest in helping our community.
- We were both interested in growing as people. This was the one
  area in which we clicked the most. He and I both used to think
  of life beyond the field. We talked about different religions and
  philosophies, and at times our talks would last for hours. We

exchanged a lot of ideas about how we could become better people that made a difference in the lives of others.

It was for those reasons that after a month of being on the same team we asked the club to allow us to be roommates for road games. He usually got up before me on the road because he liked to go out and eat breakfast, take a walk, and get some fresh air, whereas I only left our room for team meetings and team meals. On this morning there was no team breakfast scheduled, so when I got up I ordered room service, and then I waited for Pat to come back to the room.

Since being drafted by Seattle things had gone extremely well for me and for the club. In my first season I had scored four goals and had four assists, not bad for a rookie. But I was more pleased with the fact that I had cemented myself as a starting player on one of the best teams in the league and that I had become someone the team could count on to deliver when it mattered. We made the MLS playoffs and won the U.S. Open Cup in my first year, which were both good achievements in and of themselves, but when you factor in that my first year was also the team's first year as an MLS club it made our achievements that much more impressive. In my second year we got even better.

After a slow start to the season we became the best team in the league during the second half of the year as we won ten of our final fifteen games, tying three and losing just two. One of those losses came when our playoff status had already been secured. It was in our last regular season game, an away game against Houston. We played some amazing football in the second half of that 2010 season and I would say it was the most enjoyable period of my career. I've always enjoyed playing, but during that specific period I was having more fun than ever before. We had a great team spirit in our locker room, and we had the right amount of confidence without every crossing the line into arrogance. Our self-confidence may have come across as arrogant to those on the outside, but to those of us on the inside we knew that we had a good thing going and we had every reason to believe in ourselves. From top to bottom we had a solid team. Our usual starting lineup during that run was:

Keller

Riley   Hurtado   Parke   Gonzales

Nyassi   Evans   Alonso   Zakuani

Montero   Nkufo

With Kasey Keller in goal we never had to worry about anything. During my first ever practice with the team the first thing I noticed was just how good Kasey was. I'd watched him play in England when I was growing up but I hadn't realized how good he was until I tried to score against him in training.

Our defense was pretty solid, all four of them were good enough athletes to keep up with the best forwards in the league, and they also helped us start our attacks from the back.

On the wing Sanna Nyassi was phenomenal for us during the second half of the 2010 season. He was as fast as anyone in the league, and once he added the ability to score goals to his game he became a very dangerous player.

Brad Evans and Osvaldo Alonso dominated the midfield in all of our games. Brad was just an all around good player. I wouldn't say he was exceptional at any one thing; he was very accomplished in all areas. His ability to quickly transition from offense to defense was huge for us because we often attacked with a lot of players who weren't always keen on getting back to defend, and Brad provided a good balance between our offense and our defense.

When Brad was injured for a part of the year, Nathan Sturgis, who also did a great job for us, replaced him in the lineup. Sturgis wasn't the most athletic guy, but he had great close control and passing ability. Alonso—or Ozzie, as we called him—well, I don't know what I can say about him other than he was the best all-around player I have ever played with. I think he has been the best player in MLS for the last few years, and without him we would never have won half the amount of games that we won. He and I had a very good understanding on the field. We loved playing together, and he always knew how to find my runs.

Our forwards were both exceptional. Blaise Nkufo was a tremendous goal scorer. He came to us at the twilight of his career, but he was still very good. He spoke French because he was originally from the

Congo and had grown up in Switzerland—both are French-speaking countries—and we connected right away and became very good friends. Fredy Montero was just a special player; there is no other way to describe him. We had both arrived in Seattle at the same time, and from the onset he had hugely impressed me. He had a tendency to drift in and out of games at times or suffer a loss of form for a few weeks, but when he was on there was just no stopping him. He could score in every way: left foot, right foot, in the box, outside the box, headers, free kicks—Fredy was brilliant.

What made us almost unbeatable during that run was that our whole team was playing well. It's no use having good players who are in bad form. We had good players in good form and that was the key to our success. We went into games knowing we would win, and more often than not we did. We were consistently beating teams by two or three goals, and it didn't matter whether we were playing at home or on the road, we were always the better team. We were dominating most of our games from start to finish, and the best thing about us was that the team was the star. Don't get me wrong. We had some very good players who were having great individual seasons, but our biggest strength was that we all played for the team.

It was in that 2010 season, my second professional one, that I scored the two best goals of my career. The second best goal of my career was in a game at home against the New England Revolution. Leo Gonzalez, our left back, took a long throw-in that found its way to the feet of Brad Evans. Brad took two touches, and with his second he flicked the ball high into the air in my direction. As I watched the ball fall out of the sky I got my feet set, ran onto the ball, and met it with a perfect shot before it hit the ground. Bang!!! The ball flew off my foot, hit the crossbar, and bounced into the net. I could hardly believe it; it was a perfect goal. The place went nuts as I ran off to celebrate with my teammates.

The feeling I used to get from scoring a goal in front of the Sounders' fans is indescribable. It was beyond goose bumps, and beyond getting the chills. It was always a very special moment and I would probably say that it was never more special than when I scored the very best goal of my career in a late-season game at home against Chivas USA.

We were in the midst of our incredible run, and heading into this game our only goal was to keep the run going. There was a good atmosphere inside the stadium as this was our last regular season home game. The place was buzzing with excitement. As the game started my first few touches of the ball were not very good, so I decided that the next time the ball came to me I would keep it simple. I would control it and then pass it so I could get my touch and my confidence going. But football is a funny old game and it hardly ever goes according to any one person's plan. Jeff Parke, our center back, won the ball from a Chivas player and passed it to me. I thought to myself, Just control it, and then pass it, Steve. But as soon as I controlled it the game opened up and I saw a direct path to goal. I dribbled by three or four defenders in the blink of an eye, and all of a sudden I was face to face with their goalkeeper, Zach Thornton. He was a really big guy, and because I didn't think I could hit the ball by him without him saving it I decided to dribble it around him and pass it into an empty net. It was my tenth goal of the year, and the best one of my career.

Needless to say, the crowd erupted as I sped off to celebrate with my teammates. That goal was the kind of goal I would dream about scoring when I was a kid lying on my bed at night. My friends and I used to call that kind of goal a "FIFA goal" because it was the type of goal you usually only saw in a videogame.

At the end of that second season we repeated as U.S. Open Cup winners and once again made the playoffs, only to be defeated by the Los Angeles Galaxy in the first round. That defeat to L.A. was a massive black spot on an otherwise great season. That's the disadvantage of the MLS system when you compare it to the European system. You can be amazing throughout the MLS regular season, but it's only the playoffs that count. No one ever remembers the best team in the regular season, only the MLS Cup Champions. In Europe, there are no playoffs, the team with the best regular season record is crowned champion.

After the season my birth country, the Democratic Republic of Congo, selected me to play for them in a friendly game against Mali. I accepted the invitation because it was only a friendly game and not an official competitive one. Playing in a friendly game didn't tie me down to the Congo national team, which meant that if one day down the line I wanted to play for the U.S. I would still be eligible to do so. At the time I was about three years away from receiving my U.S. citizenship. I never considered playing for England for the simple fact that I knew I would never get selected. I'll always be English, but when it came to football my approach was that I would play where I had the best chance of having the most success. And after living in the U.S. for four years at that point and having gone thorough the college system to get to the pros, I felt very much a part of the American soccer system. I would have chosen the U.S. over the Congo if it had come down to it, but that's not to say that it wasn't a huge honor to have played in that exhibition game for the Congo.

To play for the country I was born in, the country that my entire family came from, was a great accomplishment. I am not an overly emotional person but I did get close to tearing up as we sang the national anthem before the game. We lost that game 3-1 to Mali. I played sixty minutes and I helped assist our goal on the night. The game was played in France, just outside of Paris, so the next morning I took the train from Paris to London so I could rest at home for a few days before I had to head up north to Liverpool, where I was scheduled to spend the following week training with Everton, one of the best teams in England.

It was a really busy offseason, one that filled me with extreme confidence heading into my third year with the Sounders. I had played a game at the international level, I had spent some time practicing with a very good team, Everton, and I had experienced a great season the year before. I was getting better, more confident, and I felt that I was primed to have an even better year than the one I'd had the previous season. Those were all the things on my mind as I headed into training camp in preparation for the 2011 season. I was truly convinced that I was about to enter a phase of my career when I would play my best football. I couldn't have been more excited to get the season started.

Pat walked back into the room just as I was getting out of the shower. We talked for a little while, and then we watched some TV. We were in Denver for a game against the Colorado Rapids that evening and we were both just trying to relax in the hours leading up to kickoff. I had reached a point in my career where I knew what it was that I needed to do in order to get myself ready to play well. I had played in over seventy professional games in just two years, so I had already gained a lot of experience and knowledge of what it took to get myself ready, or in the zone.

I knew that as long as I stayed relaxed until an hour or so before the game started my body would be in the right place, and so would my mind. In the hours leading up to any given game I listened to a lot of relaxing music, sometimes jazz, but usually R&B. I would listen to Alicia Keys, Leona Lewis, Adele, and other artists like that.

On some days I read a book or took a nap. Once in a while before a game I would turn my laptop on and watch Thierry Henry or Ronaldinho videos on YouTube for inspiration. Those were two of the best players ever and watching their highlights always inspired me.

As we got to within an hour of kickoff in the locker room I began psyching myself up by playing some up-tempo rap music that would get my adrenaline going. This routine of going from a completely relaxed state to getting myself completely pumped up just before the game started was the formula that I needed to make sure I was in the right frame of mind to have a good game.

Of course, in every game there are things that you aren't able to control, like the referee, the level of performance your opponent gives, the weather, and so on and so forth. But when it came to the things that I could control, like my preparation and my mind state, I made sure that I always stayed on top of things.

Playing Colorado wasn't going to be an easy game, but I felt that we were turning the corner after our slow start to the season, winning only once in our first five games. This was a nationally televised game and it was a good opportunity for us to show America that we were better than our present record suggested. I'd already scored two goals on the year and was hoping to add another one that evening. I wasn't the type of player that sets a target for how many goals or assists he wants to have. The only goals I set from year to year were along the lines of:

- Improve my crossing.
- Work on shooting everyday.
- Work on my heading. (This never improved, I was terrible in the air!)
- Spend time developing more skills I can use around the box.

The goals I set myself were for improvement in the different areas of my game. I always felt that if I was constantly improving, the goals and assists would become natural byproducts of my improvement.

Before my injuries I got better every year, and a large part of that was because of the time I spent working on specific parts of my game.

After my first year, when I had scored four goals, my coach, Sigi, told me that he wanted me to score more goals the following year. At the start of the 2010 season, once team practice was over, I worked on my finishing with Sigi every day. I shot about fifty balls a day for several weeks. My production went up from four goals to eleven. I worked on my shooting, and the goals came as a byproduct of that.

Patrick and I both liked to take a shower before every game and it was no different on this night. He went first and as I waited for him to finish, I channel surfed and listened to music. Once Patrick finished taking his shower, I went in to the bathroom to get myself ready. Shower. Shave. Stretch. Even though I'd already showered that morning and hadn't done much of anything since I still took a pregame shower because that was a part of my routine. Shower time was thinking time. It was a good time to start thinking about the game and to start visualizing myself doing well in it.

After my shower I got dressed and headed down to the team bus. I don't remember much about the drive to the stadium or anything that took place in the locker room before the game. My memory picks back up at the point when both teams were standing in the tunnel ready to go out onto the pitch and do battle.

The weather was just perfect, not too hot and not too cold. The slight breeze was a welcome addition as well because the worst thing about playing in Colorado was always the altitude, which made it very hard to breathe during the game. The altitude always made you tire much more quickly than in other games in which you did the same amount of running. With the altitude being what it was, it would have been a nightmare if we also had to contend with hot weather. Trying to run at altitude is hard enough by itself, as is trying to run in the heat. Having the two together would have been a disaster, which is why the breeze I felt as I walked out onto the field brought a smile to my face.

The grass was in great condition. It was cut low and was slightly wet, which was good for us because of our style of play. We liked to pass the ball quickly along the ground, a style that was suited to a slick, wet field rather than a dry, sticky one.

After receiving our final instructions from Sigi we were ready to get the game started. The referee blew his whistle. I took a deep breath, and then I went on my first run of the night. The start of any game is usually a bit chaotic and disorganized. It takes a game about five or ten minutes to settle down, not always, but usually. The first two minutes of this game were fast as the ball zipped around the pitch and both teams tried to establish control. I hadn't had any real involvement in the game thus far, so I decided that the next time we had control of the ball I would leave my usual position on the left of midfield to go and look for the ball. I wanted to get myself involved in the game so that I could try to make something happen. In the meantime, however, it was Colorado who were on the attack. They were attacking down their right side, our left, which was my side, and this meant that I had to help defend. I never liked defending, but I had learned that it was an important part of the game and that the team needed to defend well as a unit in order to be successful. In football you can't carry players when it comes to defending.

As I tracked back, Colorado lost possession of the ball and it went to our left back, Tyson Wahl. I immediately called for the ball and he gave it to me. I felt pressure from one of their defenders, so I rolled the ball between his legs and started to run around him. I looked up and saw open space in front of me. I loved seeing open space because it meant that I could push the ball up the field and use my speed to launch an attack for us. That's what was on my mind as I took my next touch of the ball, but before I could push it up field I felt a forceful tackle to my right leg.

Bang!

And then I heard a loud pop.

Everyone else heard it too. I could see it in their faces.

I fell to the ground and landed on my back.

I looked around: the referee was rushing toward me, as were some of my teammates. Even players on the Colorado bench were up on their feet looking concerned. I looked at my right leg and knew instantly what had happened. I had seen it happen to others before, on television, and it wasn't a pretty sight. My lower leg was bent in two directions. I had broken it. A broken leg is one of those injuries that every footballer fears. I would take a hundred muscle tears before I asked for a broken leg. The whole stadium was silent because even the fans could see that something out of the ordinary had taken place. There was a collective sense of shock that filled the air.

Everything seemed to be happening in slow motion. Both sets of team trainers ran onto the field. My teammates were pushing and shoving the player who had tackled me, and the referee and his assistants were trying to bring things to order. My season is over, I thought to myself. It was April, and based on the history of the players I had seen suffer this injury before it would take about a year before I would be anywhere near close to returning to the pitch. The MLS season ended in late November, so I knew I had no realistic chance of being back that season. My season is over. I felt helpless.

I was lifted onto a stretcher and carried off the field; every fan in the stands applauded me. It was a nice touch from both sets of fans, and it was one of those moments when we were all reminded that life goes beyond sports. We all want to win, compete, and be the best, but that competitive spirit is checked at the door when someone's health is threatened. Seeing anyone get hurt in a serious way will put things in perspective quickly for any of us.

I was incredibly calm in the immediate aftermath of the incident because I was very quick to accept what had happened. My leg was broken, my season was over, and I would have a massive uphill fight if I harbored hopes of ever playing again. I accepted that grim reality right off the bat. Those were the facts, I couldn't change them, and so I didn't try. I have no idea what any of my teammates, the Colorado players, or my team trainers said to me as I was carried off the field because my mind was consumed with the realization that I had played my last game of that season. The 2011 MLS season, one that I had worked extremely hard preparing for and had looked forward to with childlike enthusiasm, was over for me. I was stretchered off and placed in an ambulance that was just off to the side of the field. I heard the whistle blow and the game resumed. Just like that, life went on.

As I lay in the ambulance the doors were open and I could see the game going on. I was watching it as if I was a fan in the stands and I didn't like the experience one bit. I'm supposed to be out there, this is my game. I cringed at the thought of going through this sort of thing for the next year or more; watching a game that I knew I should have been playing in was pure torture!

The paramedics asked me a few basic questions as they hooked me up to an IV. Our assistant team trainer, Chris Cornish, was in the

ambulance with me and so was the Colorado Rapids team chaplain.
The chaplain said a few encouraging words to me, and then he prayed
for me before he exited the ambulance. I stopped watching the game
and just closed my eyes as I tried escape and forget what had just happened. Of course, it didn't work. There was just no escaping the reality
of the situation: I may never play football again.

It was while we were driving to the hospital that it began. Without
warning, the worst physical pain I had ever felt in my life kicked in. My
leg began to throb and it felt as if it was going to explode. From the
moment I was tackled I'd felt a bit of discomfort but it had been manage-
able. The feeling had been more numb and tingly than painful. But now
I was on the verge of tears because of how bad it hurt. I looked at Chris
and told him that the pain was becoming unbearable. In his English
accent, he replied, "I know mate, I know. We're almost at the hospital."

Even though the driver had the siren on and was doing his best to
weave in and out of the evening traffic, in my head I was yelling at him
with passion, "Come on, man, drive fast!" As the throbbing got worse
so did the yelling in my head, "Drive, man, drive! I'm dying back here."
I couldn't believe that anything could hurt so much. Eventually I did
say something out loud to the driver, "How long left until we're there?"
When he turned and replied, "Just another minute," I was finally able
to relax a little. I bit down on my jersey to stop myself from screaming,
placed my hands over my face, and took a deep breath.

Once I arrived at the hospital I was quickly wheeled into a room
where I was given some morphine to help ease my pain. As I waited
for a doctor to come and check on me I realized that I was still in my
uniform. Not only did I have my jersey, shorts, and socks on, but I
also still had my boots and shin guards on. I looked at Chris and said,
"Since I'm still in my uniform, do you think I can make it back for the
second half?" We both laughed.

As soon as he walked in the doctor told me that they were going
to have to cut my right boot off so that they could properly examine
my leg. *Don't you dare touch my boots, man. I like these ones. They're white,
they're brand new, and I feel fast in them. Don't touch my boots, bro. Besides,
what is there to examine? My leg broke, end of story. It doesn't need to be examined.* Those are all the things I was dying to say, but instead, through
clenched teeth, I said, "Sure, go ahead and cut them." I then watched
in horror as my new Adidas F50 boot got cut into pieces and thrown

into the trash. In that moment I silently wondered how long it would be before I would be able to wear football boots again.

After calling the Sounders' team doctor, Dr. Morris, to consult on some things, the doctor decided that I should get surgery right away. Dressed in my shorts, socks, and jersey, I was taken into the operating room, where I was given anesthesia. I instantly began to feel drowsy, and the last thing I remember before passing out was Chris telling me that we were winning 1-0. Fredy Montero had scored. I smiled and passed out. I remained unconscious for the next few hours as the doctors at the Rose Medical Centre in Denver, Colorado, tried to fix my leg and save my career.

When I awoke from my surgery I was in a room with Sigi and the Sounders' general manager and owner, Adrian Hanauer. Both Sigi and Adrian had stayed back with me in Denver while the rest of the team had flown back to Seattle after the game. It was nice of them to stay and it definitely wasn't something that I was expecting them to do, but as I would learn over the next few months, the entire Sounders organization was prepared to go out of their way in order to let me know that I wasn't alone in my fight to get back on the field. The depth to which the Sounders organization went out of their way to make sure I knew I wasn't alone in my fight to get back to playing will never be lost on me.

Randy Noteboom, our head trainer, also stayed back with me in Denver. I had always enjoyed a good working relationship with Randy, but over the next few months our working relationship would grow and blossom into a genuine off-field friendship as we spent countless hours together during my physical therapy sessions.

On the surface our friendship didn't really make much sense. I was in my twenties, Randy was in his fifties. I grew up in London, a busy, fast-paced city that is home to millions of people, while Randy grew up in a really small town two hours north of Seattle that no one had heard of. He liked to watch birds and read about them. I didn't. He loved to go fishing. I've never been.

But in spite of our differences we always seemed to have a lot to talk about. We argued daily about the NBA and, more specifically, LeBron James. I loved everything about LeBron, Randy hated the way he left the Cleveland Cavaliers, among other things. Randy was also my self-appointed relationship advisor. His favorite line to use on me was, "Take it slow, go real slow. You're still too young to know what love is." We got on really well, so I was really happy to see him in the room when I came around after my surgery.

My memory of that morning is somewhat foggy. I remember that I made small talk with Adrian and Sigi, but I was still too groggy from all the drugs in my system to hold any meaningful conversation. And my energy was low, so I spent most of the day sleeping. Adrian and Sigi left for Seattle sometime that afternoon, leaving Randy behind with me. I never expected my recovery from this injury to be a cakewalk. I knew that there would be setbacks and challenges in my rehab, but even with that said I never expected there to be a major complication right away. Within twenty-four hours of my surgery I was wheeled back into the operating room for the first of many surgeries that tried to correct the compartment syndrome I had developed.

In my case compartment syndrome meant that after my surgery I had developed a severe swelling in my right leg. The swelling was putting my nerves under enormous pressure, and if it wasn't released the nerves in my leg that were under that pressure would die and I would lose all feeling in my right foot. I'm not sure what the exact procedure looked like. All I know is that the doctor felt it was "of the utmost importance and urgency" that I get back on the operating table. The doctors wanted to release the swelling in my leg right, as that would take the pressure off my nerves, which would limit the possibility of me losing the control and feeling in my right foot. The thing about nerves is that once you lose them it's game over, they're gone.

Strangely enough, I had been down this nerve road once before. If you remember, in 2003, after I had crashed that moped, along with damaging my knee, I had also suffered some nerve damage. In that case I was fortunate to able to recover one hundred percent of the feeling in my foot, even though it took a very long time for that to happen. I remember how hard it was and what it felt like to have to drag my foot around because I was incapable of lifting it. If with this new injury I suffered nerve damage anywhere near what I had suffered in 2003, then there was no doubt that my career would be over.

Trying to come back from a broken leg is difficult enough as it is, but having to also worry about whether or not you'll ever regain the nerve function in your right foot makes your comeback attempt at least twice as hard. Over the next few months my biggest physical challenge as I tried to get back on the field was the fight against compartment syndrome, not my broken bones. You see, after my leg surgery my bones healed naturally and I was in control of how much work I did in the gym in order to put strength back in my leg. Nerves, on the other hand, were a whole different ball game. I had zero control over how fast they regenerated, and as long as I didn't have any control over my foot I wouldn't be able to play again.

After my first surgery for compartment syndrome, the doctors told me that they hadn't been able to completely release the swelling in my leg and so I would need to get back on the operating table for them to try again. The second surgery was also unsuccessful; in the end I needed three more surgeries before my compartment syndrome was brought under control. In total, including the very first surgery that I had immediately after the tackle, I went under the knife five times because of that one injury.

Five surgeries in a matter of weeks would take a toll on anyone. I lost eighteen pounds pretty quickly, which devastated me. I am a skinny guy to begin with, and my ideal playing weight is one hundred and sixty-five pounds. That is when I feel at my best. I was down to one hundred and forty-seven pounds within weeks of my injury because I had no appetite, I was unable to work out, and I was constantly going into the operating room. I hated the feeling the anesthesia gave me. I remember how it felt to wake up feeling drowsy and drained of all my energy after every surgery. I spent several days at a time floating in and out of sleep, unable to eat or sit up in bed. All I could do was lie there and pray that I didn't have to go through another surgery.

The first person I became close to when I got to the University of Akron was a guy named Pablo Moreira. He was a senior when I was a freshman, but that didn't stop us from developing a close relationship on and off the field. After graduating Pablo decided not to pursue a career in soccer and went into the corporate working world instead.

We stayed in touch throughout the rest of my time at Akron, and when I got to MLS he often flew out to Seattle to visit me for days at a time. He was very much like a big brother to me. When I was out of line he would tell me, when I needed an arm around my shoulder after a tough loss he provided it, and when I wanted some advice on important decisions in my life Pablo was always on hand to offer it.

At the time of my injury he was working for a company in Denver, and having seen my injury on TV he decided to come to the hospital and pay me a visit. At the exact same time, the Sounders had flown both of my parents out to Denver, and so on my third day post-injury I was in very good company with Pablo and my parents in town. Having them there helped to take my mind off of what I was going through. I was able to laugh for the first time in days, and it was good to be able to share any fears and concerns I had with people I trusted.

I was in Denver for about five days before it was decided that I needed to head back to Seattle so that I could be under the care of the Sounders' medical team going forward. Pablo stayed in Denver and my dad flew back to London. Randy, my mom, and I got ready to fly to Seattle. I was in no condition to fly commercially since I couldn't bend my right leg yet, so Adrian got me a private jet instead. It was an incredible act of kindness and it allowed me to fly back in comfort because I was able to keep my leg straight by putting my feet up on the chair facing me. I had never flown on a private jet before, and although I wish that my first time had been under different circumstances, let's not kid ourselves, broken leg or not, a private jet is a private jet.

One of the benefits of flying private is that you normally fly out of smaller airports and you avoid all of the security checks and long lines that come with flying commercial. In my condition there was no way I would have been able to withstand the long lines that you find at a normal airport. I wasn't strong enough to use crutches yet, so I ~~forced~~ asked Randy to push me around the airport in a wheelchair. While he was complaining I told him that he should be thanking me for giving him a chance to get in some good exercise in his old age. "You're not getting any younger. You should be grateful for all the exercise you can get at this point." He pushed me all the way across the tarmac and right up to the plane, and that was when we encountered a problem.

It was a small plane, and the only way to get on it was to walk up the steps. I think there were about three steps in total, and there was no wheelchair ramp. With no crutches, no wheelchair ramp, and with me not being able to walk, we had no idea how I was going to get on the plane. While Randy and I went back and forth trying to work something out, the two pilots came up to me and asked, "How much do you weigh?" Before I could answer them, one of them went behind me and placed his arms under my armpits while the other one held my legs. They then lifted me off the wheelchair, up the steps, and onto the plane. They carried me all the way to the backseat before setting me down. I high-fived and thanked them both before I turned to Randy and said, "You should be ashamed of yourself for letting the pilots do all that work. What if they have no strength left to fly the plane?"

We flew with the cockpit door open because I wanted to have the same view that the pilots had, and I also wanted to be able to ask them any questions that came to mind. I've been in love with planes since before I can remember, so any time I get a chance to pick a pilot's brain I take it. I'm not sure exactly what it is about planes that I love, but the idea of one day flying one excites me, and it would be the first item on my bucket list if I had one.

Between the Rose Medical Center in Denver and Virginia Mason in Seattle I spent a little over two weeks in hospitals before I was discharged and sent home. Once I got home the fight to get fit began. As I began what would become a five hundred day journey to get back into the Sounders' starting lineup there were many high and low points. If I tried to write about everything I experienced in that five hundred day journey I would need to write three books, and so I've decided to write about a few of the high moments and a few of the low ones that I encountered on my journey. A lot of this material came from the journals I kept during that time, so this is me being as vulnerable as I can be in the hopes that the things I went through and wrestled with can give you the inspiration you need to overcome any adversity you might be facing. And I hope that as you read about my high points you'll see that even in the midst of terrible seasons in our lives there is always a silver lining.

THE HIGH POINTS

The Sounders Organization

I've already given a couple of examples of how the Sounders took care of me during my rehab phase: flying my parents out and providing me with a jet are two huge ways in which they helped me, but there were smaller everyday things they did that made a difference in my life.

One time, after a game that I watched from a suite because I was still injured, I made my way into the players lounge to congratulate the guys on a good win that night. As I made my way through the crowd that had gathered in the lounge I bumped into Adrian, our general manager and owner.

"Steve, it's good to see you," he said as we shook hands.

"Good to see you too, Adrian"

"How are you holding up?" he asked.

"I'm hanging in there. I've had better days." I always tried to be honest with Adrian throughout my time in Seattle.

"Yeah, I bet. Anything the club can do to help?"

"Umm, not really. I can't think of anything at this point," I felt like Adrian and the Sounders had already done so much for me at that point that I didn't feel right asking for anything else.

"How are you doing mentally?"

"That's the biggest battle," I confessed.

"Okay, well listen. If you ever need to get away for a couple of days just let me know. You can use my plane and fly to Mexico. I have a place for you to stay while you're there. Just say the word and it's a done deal."

"Wow, thanks. I'll definitely keep that in mind."

I never said the word, so I never took advantage of that offer, but it was an incredible thing for Adrian to do. A few months after that I told my teammate Brad Evans that story and his reply was, "You're a fool. I would have been on that plane the next day!" I couldn't disagree with him. Throughout my five years with Seattle I always found Adrian to be a great GM, and he was especially great during my fight to get back on the pitch.

Sounders Fans

What can I say that hasn't already been said about this special group of people? From day one the Sounders' fans embraced me and made me feel very welcome. But their affection and support went up to a whole new level when I suffered my injury. I literally received over five thousand letters of encouragement from them, and any time I bumped into fans on the streets they would wish me well. One time I ordered a pizza and the delivery guy happened to be a Sounders fan. We ended up talking about football and the Sounders in my hallway for about ten minutes.

The most precious thing the fans ever did for me, though, was during a game I didn't even play in. The first game the team played after my injury was against Toronto FC in Seattle. I was lying in a hospital bed just a couple of miles away from where the game was taking place. Two of my good friends, David and Stephen, visited me in the hospital that afternoon and as we were talking I asked them to take my mom to the game that night because I felt that it would be good for her to get out of the hospital. She had refused to leave my side ever since she'd arrived in the U.S., and even though I had a warm bed waiting for her at home she chose to sleep on a pullout mattress on the hospital floor every night.

Anyway, during the game that night at the eleventh-minute mark, the entire stadium, forty thousand people, lifted up white cards with my jersey number—11—printed on them. They held the cards up and proceeded to chant my name for the entire minute even though the game was still going on. My mom broke down and cried. I actually never saw it happen live. I had the game playing in my hospital room but I had fallen asleep after only a couple of minutes. I watched the YouTube clip of that moment a few days later, and as I heard the "STEVE . . . ZAKUANI" chants I shed a few tears. Even now as I write these words I'm overcome with emotion. It was the most special thing the fans ever did for me, and to this day all around Seattle people still have those white cards hanging on their bedroom walls or in the back windows of their cars. Every time I see one of them I'm reminded of the support the Sounders' fans gave my family and me during the worst moment of my life.

My Support System

I would not have made it back onto the pitch had it not been for the people I had around me. Both my parents dropped everything they were doing and flew to Denver as soon as it happened. That in and of itself was enough to show me that I wouldn't tackle this fight alone. My dad is not usually an emotional man, but on the day he flew back to London from Denver he held my hand and told me he was rooting for me to get through this injury. Once I saw the tears in his eyes I couldn't help but shed a few tears, too.

My mom, well, she was superwoman throughout the entire process. I was on about four different medications that I had to take at specific times on a twenty-four-hour cycle. My mom wrote out a schedule and set multiple alarms to remind her when it was time for me to take my medication. Sometimes I would need to take a certain pain med at two in the morning but I would be fast asleep. My mom would come out of her room, wake me up, give me my meds, and then go back to sleep. Two hours later she would repeat that cycle. She was also with me, along with my agent Rich, when I made my first public appearance at a Sounders game following my injury as I sat in a suite watching the Sounders play against the Vancouver Whitecaps in the summer of 2012. There aren't enough words in any language to thank my parents for their sacrifices during that time.

As if visiting me in hospital in Denver wasn't enough, Pablo also flew to Seattle for a few days after my mom had left to make sure I was doing okay. At the time I was often too weak to get up and go to the bathroom, so I would urinate in some kind of hospital-provided bottle that needed to be emptied after each use. It was one thing to see my mom take my pee bottle and empty it several times a day, that's what moms do; but to see my friend Pablo hold my pee in his hands and empty the bottle for me, that was a whole other thing. He was my driver and my errand boy as well for the time he was with me. Anything that I needed done, he did. A short time after that Pablo became a coach with the Portland Timbers, and so when I was traded to the Timbers we got to work together and live in the same city again.

I used to go to Mr. Goodison's house to be mentored every Wednesday for a whole year shortly after he had to taken me to hear Myles Munroe speak and there were a few other boys that went with me. Two of them became my closest friends on this planet.

Serge is actually my cousin but I consider him a brother first. We grew up together, and in our late teens we became very close, as we both got very interested in reading books and trying to better our lives. Serge's best friend growing up was a guy called Andrey. I had known Andrey through Serge for many years. We'd all gone to the same school, but once we began attending the weekly meetings at Mr. Goodison's house Andrey and I developed our own friendship.

We became inseparable to the point that there were times when we would talk on the phone for nine straight hours. On a couple of occasions we even fell asleep while on the phone to each other. All of our conversations were about how we could change the world and make a difference. We used to spend hours talking about taking the lessons we had learned from Myles Munroe and Mr. Goodison and using them to help other people realize their dreams. Those conversations eventually led to what became Kingdom Hope, the organization I founded in 2010.

The reason these two guys were important for me during my rehab was that when I talked with them we would talk about any and every thing except football. I was getting hundreds of messages every week from people asking me about my injury. I was doing interviews about it, and everywhere I went I couldn't escape being reminded of my leg and of my injury. It was nice to be able to have a place where I could escape escape and not have to think about my injury. With Serge and Andrey I was able to laugh, free my mind, and forget about football every once in a while.

Fans from all over MLS also played a huge role in helping me cope with everything that was going on. The Colorado Rapids, the team I had been injured against, sent me a giant get well soon card, and some other MLS teams also sent me their best wishes. On my Facebook and Twitter accounts I was flooded with messages of support from non-Sounder fans. It was really touching to read all of the nice things that fans that normally rooted against me were saying. The Seattle Mariners baseball team also reached out to me when they sent me a signed ball and a card.

When I went to Arizona with the Sounders for training camp in 2012, I met two very special ladies. I had known Renee for a couple of years through social media but I had never met her in person. She was a huge fan of mine and she always sent me messages of support online. Renee and her wife, Charlene, live in Arizona and so when they found out that I would be down there, they drove a few hours to come and see me at practice. There's not much I can say about that level of support except that it gave me added motivation to return to the pitch so that they could watch me play again.

My fiancée and I have become very good friends with them and to this day, their unconditional support still inspires me in many ways.

Two footballers who I admired when I was growing up made a huge impact on me during my rehab phase. The first is David Beckham, and the second is Thierry Henry. When I was lying on my hospital bed in Denver I opened my email one night and saw that I had received a message from an account that I didn't recognize. When I began reading the message I realized that it was from David Beckham.

He was the first person to reach out and it was a really touching message. He had just recovered from a potentially career-ending Achilles injury himself, so he was very well placed to offer advice on how best to overcome what I was going through. We exchanged a few emails over the next few months and a lot of the advice that he gave me helped me keep a positive mindset even when I faced some incredible odds.

Thierry Henry was the king of the English Premier League when I was growing up. I was in the Arsenal youth academy when he was dominating for the Arsenal first team and I used to sit in the stands watching him in awe every weekend. Growing up every kid in the neighborhood wanted to be Thierry Henry; he was just that good. The first time I met him was in 2009 when he was playing for Barcelona and the Sounders played an exhibition game against them. He was a good friend of my teammate Freddie Ljungberg (they had played together for eight years at Arsenal), so I asked Freddie to introduce me, which he did. The following year, Thierry came to MLS when he signed with the New York Red Bulls.

When they came to play in Seattle I was injured and he was suspended. He had gotten a red card a few days earlier when New York had played Portland, but rather than return to the East Coast he had stayed with his team in the Pacific Northwest. I arranged to meet him at his hotel the night before the game and we ended up having dinner and a three-hour conversation. I won't lie and say that during dinner there weren't times when I had to pinch myself and say, "Wait, am I really having dinner with Thierry Henry?" I used to play with him on FIFA when I was kid and I always pretended to be him when I played football on the school playground with my friends. It was definitely a surreal experience. But over time, as we talked more and more, Thierry became someone who was always ready to give me advice and encouragement. He had seen players come back from all kinds of injuries and he assured me that I would be back eventually. When I texted him to talk about this book and my decision to retire he was supportive and some of the encouragement he shared with me are printed on the front cover of this book.

I obviously can't name every single person who helped me and reached out to me because there so were many people who made small gestures that I've probably already forgotten about, but that's not to say I wasn't extremely grateful to them. I was, I am, and I always will be!

Dr. Myles Munroe

From the moment I first heard Dr. Myles Munroe speak, I knew I had met someone special. In the months and years following that day I read dozens of his books and downloaded hundreds of his leadership presentations. I did a lot of research on him and found out that he was a pastor, a businessman, a government consultant, and an author. He traveled all over the world teaching people how to become leaders. I watched a lot of his online seminars and wished that one day I could sit in a room and have a conversation with him. Although I had seen him speak in person many times I had never officially met him.

In December 2010 I decided to fly to the Bahamas to try and meet Myles Munroe. I booked a ticket and a hotel and I flew out the next day. Upon arriving in the Bahamas I found out that everyone knew who he was. Whenever people asked me the reason for my visit and I told them that I was there to meet Myles Munroe, they knew exactly who I was talking about.

On my first day in the Bahamas I went to his organization's headquarters only to find out that he wasn't there. I came back the next day and after entering the lobby I spoke to a lady who worked there. She explained to me that Myles Munroe was a very busy man and that because of his travel schedule he was hardly ever in the office. I asked her to call his office anyway to at least check and see if he was there that day. To her surprise he was right upstairs, and after she told him that I had flown all the way from Seattle just to meet him he agreed to see me. I was escorted to a waiting area outside of his office and after about ten minutes Myles Munroe appeared.

I have met a lot of celebrities and famous people before and not once have I ever felt nervous or in awe. People very rarely overwhelm me, but when I saw Myles Munroe standing two feet away from me I began to tremble. Standing before me was the man whose words had changed the course of my life. The ways in which his books had influenced me were innumerable. I was overcome with emotion. My legs shook as I stayed glued to my chair. I feared that if I tried to stand up I would fall over. "You . . . you . . . you changed my life, sir . . . and I . . . I wanted . . . to fly . . . I flew here to tell . . . I want to thank you for changing my life."

Sensing my nervousness, Myles Munroe smiled and placed his hand on my shoulder. I told him my entire life story in just a few minutes and after hearing how much he had impacted me he agreed to have breakfast with me the next day. We met at the Hilton hotel on Cable Beach but I never ate. I ordered an orange juice and then spent the rest of the time asking him questions. After that meeting we stayed in touch.

Over the years that have followed I have been privileged enough to travel with him to his different speaking engagements and I've dined with him in his home on more than one occasion. One year I even spent Christmas in the Bahamas visiting him and his family. I've been around Myles Munroe more than most people have and I've seen firsthand how busy he is. But shortly after my injury, when I was with him in North Carolina, he told me that any time I felt down or afraid of what was to come I should call him to talk. I would do just that. The next year, during my rehab, we talked quite a bit, and a lot of those conversations left me as inspired as I was the first time I heard him speak.

THE LOW MOMENTS

Mental Anguish

The worst thing I dealt with in the five hundred days I fought to get back into the Sounders' starting lineup was not the multiple surgeries or the grueling hours I spent rehabbing in the gym, it was the fight between my ears. Trying to keep my mind positive and hopeful was the biggest challenge. There's just no way to prepare for a career-changing event like having your leg broken and needing five surgeries. You can't prepare for it, you can only try to bounce back from it. Some days I would come home from the gym and be feeling good about myself. I would say to myself, "You made some good progress today, you're getting there," and then a voice would whisper to me, "Oh, please! Who are you kidding? You know you're still limping and you'll never be as fast as you used to be!"

There were times when it was impossible to shut that voice up. I always did my best to remain upbeat and have a positive outlook, but there were definitely some days when the mental fight got the best of me. I would be so drained from the fear that the work I was doing in the gym was pointless and from the doubts over whether or not I would ever step foot on the field again that there were days when I passed out on my couch at six o'clock—from exhaustion!

Being unable to complete simple everyday tasks also took a mental toll on me. One day I decided to go to Target to buy some toiletries, and when I got there I realized that I wouldn't be able to carry my items because I was on crutches. I had to use a motorized shopping cart. Going from being an athlete who was capable of running down the field at lightning speed to someone who wasn't able to carry his toiletries around a store was extremely difficult to accept.

My First Week Back in Training After My Injury

You would think that I would have been ecstatic during the first week I was cleared to practice with the team. After all, wasn't that the biggest step I had taken to date? The crutches were gone, the restrictions were gone, and I was finally free to practice with the team. The truth is my first week back was a disaster. Mentally I was shot. I felt so slow and out of shape that I doubted I would ever be able to work hard enough to catch back up to my teammates. Things that I used to do so easily, that had come so naturally to me before, were now proving too difficult for me to pull off. I used to run by guys for fun in practice, but now I wasn't able to accelerate past anyone. I felt horrible.

Jeff Parke, one of my veteran teammates at the time, sensed my frustration after one practice and he took me aside. "Zak, it's gonna take a while buddy, you can't get frustrated. No one here is expecting you to step back in and start killing it right away. Don't put that pressure on yourself just yet; take baby steps." The following week was much better as I adjusted my expectation level and kept Jeff's advice in mind. I celebrated every time I made a simple pass, and when I made a mistake I told myself that it was better to be out on the field making mistakes than to be in a wheelchair in Denver being pushed around by Randy.

My First Time Watching a Sounders Game After the Injury

The Sounders were playing Sporting Kansas City in Seattle. I hadn't been to a game or a practice since my injury. I had asked Sigi to allow me to do my rehab at home because I found being around the team and the practice facility too difficult to deal with emotionally. After isolating myself for a few weeks I felt that I was ready to go and watch a game in person. My good friend and former Akron teammate Teal Bunbury was playing for Sporting at the time, and his sister, Kylie Bunbury, had flown in for the game. She was a good friend of mine, so I decided to watch the game with her and a few other friends in a suite.

As soon as the whistle blew and I heard the fans cheering I knew I wouldn't last long. I didn't belong in a suite. I was supposed to be out there on the field playing to those cheers I could hear. It wasn't fair for me to have to sit in a suite and watch a game that I should have been playing in. In that moment I hated everything about my injury. I hated the fact that it had happened, I hated the fact that I'd had multiple surgeries, and I hated the fact that I had to use crutches to walk around. I was pissed off as I sat and tried to watch the game. Although I was dying to leave I managed to stay in my seat for the whole game, but I rarely ever looked up as I spent the rest of the game texting and playing games on my phone. That night when I got home I threw one of my crutches against the wall in a moment of pure anger and frustration. I then buried my head in a pillow and passed out.

As you can see, emotionally it was a rollercoaster ride at times. I don't care how positive a person you are; when you face tremendous adversity there are times when you will feel like giving up. I felt that way many times.

Rather than drive into the practice facility to do my physical therapy every day, I chose to do it at my apartment. I didn't want to be at practice where I would see everything I was missing. It would be too difficult for me. My physical therapist was a guy named Boris Gladun and he was a pleasure to work with. At first I used to hate the sound of his knock at my door. He always arrived at around nine in the morning, and I never looked forward to him coming because the exercises that he made me do seemed so mundane. I considered myself a high-level athlete, capable of amazing physical feats, but with Boris, in the beginning at least, I was reduced to sitting on the floor as he moved my toes back and forth. It seemed like a waste of my time, but that's because I simply wasn't used to being so limited with my body. Boris continuously assured me that he was building me up slowly because I needed to re-master the basics before I could ever dream of one day being the Steve Zakuani that I used to be.

As my leg got stronger and my nerve function began to return Boris elevated my workload. He was the one who taught me how to walk with two crutches, and then one crutch, and then zero crutches. Every time I hit a new milestone my confidence in Boris increased. We got on really well, and aside from the fact that he was also an Arsenal fan I really enjoyed hearing the stories he shared with me about his journey from Russia to America.

When I first met him I didn't think he necessarily looked Russian, but once I engaged him in conversation his accent gave him away. I worked with Boris until I was able to bear my full weight on my leg and begin jogging slowly. Without Boris I would have never been able to get back on the field; he played a key role in keeping my spirits up in the beginning of the rehab process and in getting me to trust my body again.

When the time for me to ramp up my rehab by working with the Sounders' trainers arrived I had to start driving to training every day again. It was weird being back with all of my teammates and to once again sit in on team meetings. It was weird because even though I was physically there with them I still felt somewhat detached from the group since when they headed out to the pitch to practice I stayed inside the gym and did work specific to my recovery program. I was a few months away from being able to join the team in partial practice. The period in which I was in the locker room and lunch room with the boys but wasn't able to practice with them was a really difficult one. I didn't feel like a footballer. I felt like a fan who had won some kind of competition that gave me special behind-the-scenes access to the Sounders without actually being a part of the team. I did everything with the team except play with them.

On Friday afternoons, when Sigi held a team meeting to talk about the next opponent, I felt as if I didn't belong in the room. All of the other players were going to be involved in the game in some way, and so the things Sigi said were pertinent to them. But me, on the other hand, I was irrelevant and of no use to the team on game day, and so I felt ridiculous sitting in on those meetings. More than a few times I asked Sigi to allow me to skip those Friday meetings, but he told me that they were mandatory for every player. He had been nice enough in allowing me to take some extended time away from the team following my injury, so I decided not to fight him on this one. In the world of sports you have to pick and choose your battles wisely.

Over the next few months I worked my butt off in the gym. After Boris I went to work with Chris and Randy, our team trainers. I spent about two months working with them in the gym and on the field. They helped me build strength in my leg and they also helped me to start jogging again. I used to walk and jog with Randy on the perimeter of the field as the team practiced. Whenever I felt tired I would look on the field and tell myself, "If you want to be back there, one more lap won't kill you."

There were days when I would get into it with Chris and Randy. I've been known to be a bit stubborn once I make my mind up about something. On some days either Chris or Randy would devise a plan for me that I didn't agree with. They would say something like, "Today you'll walk four laps and jog two. After that you'll go in the gym and ride the bike for thirty minutes." If I felt that I should be doing more I would reply with something like, "Walk four laps? Why in the world am I walking four laps? I should be jogging more. I've proven that I can jog! How will the coaches ever put me back on the field if all they see me do is walk?" Exasperated, they'd reply, "If you try to do too much too soon, you will never get back on the field. Just trust us." As much as I disagreed with them at times I always knew that they both had my best interests at heart and that they were protecting me from my own misguided urgency. Eventually I outgrew what Chris and Randy could offer me in my rehab and they passed me on to our fitness coach, Dave Tenney.

On the Sounders, whenever an injured player is on the road to recovery, before they are allowed to participate in practice with the rest of the team they have to go through some fitness sessions with Dave. Dave is the final barrier between a player being away from the team and a player being allowed to practice with the team. The fact that I was now in the hands of Dave meant that I was only one step away from being cleared to practice, but it also meant that I had a lot of fitness work ahead of me.

Dave and I got on really well. He had already played a big role in my career, turning me from a sixty-minute per game player in my rookie year to a player who was capable of playing two ninety-minute games in the space of four days by the end of my second season. He was the best at what he did, and over the next six months he would push my body to limits I never knew it could reach. On my first day with him he turned me to and said, "Zakuani, you're gonna hate me by the time I'm done with you. If you don't hate me, then I haven't done my job! But I'm also going to get you back on the field."

TRAINING WITH DAVE TENNY

I'd been through fitness sessions with Dave before, in preseason, in the offseason, and after minor injuries I'd had, and so I was somewhat prepared for what lay ahead of me as I worked with him in the final phase of my individual training. As soon as I was able to show that I could handle the workload Dave was going to put me through without breaking down I would be allowed to start training with the team again.

The two main areas Dave wanted me to improve in were my strength and my conditioning. To improve my strength we spent several hours in the gym together. I focused a lot on improving my balance and lower-body strength so that I would be able to withstand any hard tackles I'd receive if I got back on the field. I knew that once I was cleared for full training I'd have to be wary of two of my teammates in particular, Zach Scott and Patrick Ianni. Zach and Pat were both great guys, but they both tackled very hard in practice. If I was going to survive getting hit by them I would have to get my leg much stronger. I also spent a lot of time building my core strength by doing a lot of abdominal-strengthening exercises such as planks and medicine ball crunches. Those gym sessions with Dave were never fun, but I always felt a huge sense of accomplishment when he was done with me.

To improve my conditioning I had to run a lot. I don't really enjoy running unless there is a ball involved, and because Dave understood this he implemented the ball into a lot of my fitness runs. Very rarely did we ever go out on the field and just run for the sake of running. We almost always included the ball in some way. Although the fitness work was still extremely difficult, being able to have a ball at my feet made it a lot more enjoyable.

Physically speaking, working with Dave was the most challenging part of my recovery, because even though I knew I was only one step away from being back with the team I also knew that it could take me a few months to take that single step. In the end I worked with Dave from August 2011 until April 2012. I had no offseason in 2011 as I stayed in Seattle to work with Dave through the winter months. When the team returned for the new 2012 season I was able to do some activities with the group but I still spent most of my time working with Dave. We wanted to make sure I was completely ready before I was thrown back out on the field.

I was injured in April 2011, and I returned to full training with the team in May 2012—thirteen months. This is how my rehab looked month by month during that time:

MONTH	REHAB / TRAINING
April 2011	Injured in Colorado, five surgeries
May 2011	PT with Boris at home
June 2011 – July 2011	PT with Sounders trainers Chris and Randy
Aug 2011 – April 2012	Strength and conditioning with Dave
May 2012	Cleared for team training

I remember the day that I was finally cleared for full practice. I was lying on my back trying to catch my breath after a workout with Dave when Sigi walked over to me and started a conversation.

"How do you feel?"

"I'm pretty tired," I replied.

"What about overall? How do you feel in terms of your overall fitness?"

"I'm getting there. I haven't reached my top speed yet, but everything else is coming back slowly."

"Well, I've talked to Dave and he seems to think that you're ready to join the team in practice from now on."

"Yeah?" I was pleasantly surprised.

He asked me, "Do you think you're ready?"

I answered, "Yes. I'm definitely ready; it's what I've been working for."

"Okay, you'll train with the team on Monday."

I had a big smile on my face as I got ready for bed Sunday night. Right before I fell asleep, I thought to myself, "Tomorrow morning I'll be back in the team training. The work I've been doing has paid off. I'm almost there; I'm almost there."

I got tired of talking about my injury. Every single person I met on the street or talked to on Facebook wanted to talk to me about my leg. "When will you be back? How long left in your rehab? Are you going to be the same player you were before? How does your leg feel? Did it hurt when you broke it? How many surgeries did you have? Why is it taking you so long to get back on the field?" I grew extremely tired of those questions. Every person that asked me something like that only had to have that conversation one time, but I had to have it a thousand times a week. I know that everyone who asked me about my leg meant well and wanted the best for me but there were definitely times when I just wanted people to talk to me about something else because it became so draining to keep repeating myself, "I'm getting stronger, I feel good, I'll be back soon."

I even stopped talking to the press at one point because every other question that they asked me was injury-related. Again, I completely understood why my injury was the topic of conversation, but I'd reached my tipping point. I'd had enough. I asked the Sounders' media team to let the press know that I wanted to focus solely on my rehab and that I would not be doing any more interviews. The only exception I made was for a Sports Illustrated story by Grant Wahl.

More than a few times, Sigi suggested that I should think about talking to a sports psychologist to get help with the mental challenges I was facing; and even though I was tempted to do so, because anyone who is going through a difficult experience needs an outlet or an escape, I never went through with it. Rather than sit in a weekly meeting sharing my fears and struggles, I decided that my outlet would be to do more work in the community. I felt that helping those in need would give me strength in my own battle, and that proved to be true.

When word came to me that a young local kid, Jaxon Marquadt, had suffered a similar injury to mine, I decided to offer him some encouragement. I waited until he was healthy enough to start practicing with his team again, and then I showed up to his practice, unannounced, and gave him some autographed items. The shocked look on his face was priceless. His mother and coach had both done a good job of keeping my appearance a secret, Jaxon had been caught completely off-guard.

I stayed in touch with him for a few months after that as he kept me updated about his progress. Any time I was told about a kid in America who had been badly injured in a game I did my best to reach out to him or her in whatever way I could. I sent signed boots, signed scarves, emails, and even made a few phone calls.

Finding small ways in which I could use my platform to encourage others always gave me an added motivation to get back on the field, because, after all, what better hope and encouragement could I give to an injured kid than to have him or her see me running around on the field after the injury I had suffered. The best way for me to inspire anyone going through a serious injury of their own was for me to overcome my injury and return to the field. I would get the opportunity to do that a lot sooner than I had imagined.

I had been training with the team, restriction-free, for about two months before Sigi put me on the game-day roster for the first time. It was for our home game against Sporting Kansas City on June 20. There wasn't much fuss made about me being on the game-day roster. I found out the day before the game when our assistant coach, Brian Schmetzer, told me the good news, and then Sigi and I had a brief talk about it before I left the practice facility that day. I didn't tell anyone about it because even though I knew that being named as a substitute for the first time in over a year was an amazing achievement, deep down my desire was to make it back into the starting lineup; that's the goal I was working toward. The day that Sigi called me into his office to tell me I was going to be a starter again would be the day that I called my friends and family to celebrate. That day was still quite far down the line, so in the meantime I quietly congratulated myself for being named on the game-day roster, and then I set my sights on breaking into the starting lineup.

In the end I spent the entire ninety minutes against Kansas watching the game from the bench. The final score was 1-1. It was an extremely physical game with a lot of hard tackles and bad fouls; because of that, a part of me was glad that I hadn't been brought into the game. After that game our next three games were on the road. Sigi had made it clear to me that my first minutes following the injury would be in a home game so that the Sounders' fans could give me a warm reception. Sigi also said that while the team was gone for the next three weekends he felt it was best for me to stay back in Seattle to continue building my fitness. I didn't necessarily agree with his decision. I felt that I was ready to play ten, maybe fifteen minutes off the bench if the team needed it, and after getting so close to the pitch for that Kansas game not traveling with the team for the next three games felt like a demotion.

While the team was gone I split my time between the gym and the field. My latest x-rays showed that my bones had completely healed, but I was still having issues with the nerves in my foot. The sole of my right foot was extremely sensitive to the touch. When I had shoes on it felt the same as my left foot, but when I walked around the house barefoot, or when our trainers massaged it, the pain was unbearable. The sole of my foot couldn't handle direct pressure of any kind.

After every day of practice it was essential for one of our trainers to spend some time massaging the sole of my foot. Our hope was that the more physical touch my foot was exposed to the better my nerves would begin to respond to it. It was an extremely slow and painful process. Every time I sat on the treatment table for one of my foot massages I put my earbuds in and bit down on a pillow in order to stop myself from screaming. As time went on it became obvious that the biggest obstacle I'd have to overcome would not be my broken bones but the nerve complications that the compartment syndrome had caused.

Becoming a professional athlete is hard work, but remaining one is just as hard, if not harder. There is always someone out there working day and night trying to take your spot. If you want to keep your place on a professional team you have to be ready to compete and give your best effort every day. It's difficult enough to try and hold onto your spot when you are one hundred percent healthy. But when you have suffered a broken leg, had five surgeries, and are dealing with compartment syndrome it becomes ten times as hard. That reality led me to consider retirement in the summer of 2012.

Just as I was getting close to making my return to the starting lineup I began to doubt if I could ever fully overcome my injury. There were nights when I tossed and turned in bed as I tried to talk myself out of this sudden urge to retire. I don't know exactly what brought it on—maybe it was the painful foot massages or the ache I'd feel in my leg after a hard practice, but there was about a two-week period that summer when I considered telling Adrian and Sigi that I wanted to retire.

I felt that I could work hard enough to return to the field, but I was having major doubts about what I'd be capable of doing once I got there. *I knew I could be good in training, but what about in a game? Games would be the true test. Could I ever get back to feeling how I felt before? Or was the rest of my career going to be a case of playing through pain every week?* I was no longer on a level playing field with the guys I had to compete against. We all had to make sacrifices, work hard in practice, and take care of our bodies. But on top of that I now had to play with a leg that had taken five surgeries to repair and a foot that felt like it was on fire any time someone touched it. I had to work much harder than everyone else just to give myself a chance of playing. There was no escaping the reality that my body had undergone significant stress and that it would never go back to being as healthy as it was before. It was a tough pill to swallow and it brought me close to quitting. Looking back, I think I was about a week away from telling the Sounders that I was at least considering retirement.

But just before it came to that point the team returned from its three-game road trip and Sigi named me on the game-day roster for the first time since the Kansas game a few weeks earlier. This time the game was against the Colorado Rapids, the team I had been injured against.

On Friday July 6 2012, Sigi pulled me aside after practice.

"You'll be on the bench tomorrow, Steve," he told me.

"Okay, looking forward to it," I replied.

And then he said, "I know it's against Colorado, and for obvious reasons the press will make a big thing out of it. But I think you're professional enough to not let all of the storylines get in the way of your performance."

I was silent for a moment, and then I answered him, "It won't affect me. I'm glad we can get this reunion out of the way."

The next morning I woke up and tweeted, "Wake up on a high, and then I cross my heart and hope to fly." The words were taken from a song by the English rapper Wretch 32 and they were an accurate reflection of how I was feeling. I was excited about the game that night and I was praying that Sigi would give me a few minutes at the end— that was the "hope to fly" part.

In my career I was never happy about being on the bench. Before my injury I was always an automatic starter. I was one of the best players on any team I played with, and if I had to be on the bench I never took it well. But on this night, for this game, I was extremely excited to be on the bench. When I had been on the bench against Kansas a few weeks earlier I didn't think I'd be going into the game. For this game I just knew that I would. The story was too perfect for it not to happen—making my return in a nationally televised game against the team and player that had injured me—it just had to happen.

The fans are going crazy. The players on the field look distracted as they try to concentrate on playing. Even in my wildest dreams I never imagined that this would be the reception I'd receive from the fans on my return to the field. I crouch down on the sideline as I wait to be waved on by the referee. Is this really my life? The last time I played on this field was in April 2011 against Chicago, a game that I scored in. That day feels like it was in another lifetime. All those

*hours spent rehabbing with Boris, Chris, Randy, and Dave are paying off;
tonight is only the beginning.*

*I look around the stadium, I look at faces I've never seen before, and I get
chills as I see how hard they are all cheering for me. Everyone is rooting for me.
Finally, the ball goes out of play and the referee waves me on. The moment I
started praying for the second I was tackled in Colorado is here. The volume
inside the stadium goes up a couple notches. I sprint to the other side of the field
and take up my position on the left. I'm back where I belong.*

I was only on the field for five minutes and I only had four or five
touches on the ball, but as the final whistle blew I felt a big sense of
accomplishment. Those minutes I played validated all the work I had
been doing and they gave me motivation to carry on. And even though
I hadn't scored the game winner or done anything of note during the
game, all the TV cameras were following me as I walked around the
field after the game. That was another reminder that this moment, my
story, was bigger than football.

As I shook hands with the Colorado players I knew that at some
point I was going to come face to face with the player who had injured
me. I decided ahead of time that when I saw him I would trade jerseys
with him.

After a game it's very common to trade your jersey with a player
on the opposing team. Normally I only trade jerseys with my friends
or with a player that I look up to, but on this night I decided to trade
jerseys with the guy who many felt had ruined or at least drastically
slowed down my career. For months I had been telling the fans and the
press that I bore no resentment toward him, but I sensed that many
people weren't convinced by my words. The only way I would be able
to make it clear to everyone that I had forgiven him and I was ready
to move on would be through an act, because my words had not been
enough. I traded jerseys with him, gave him a hug, and then I moved on.

That moment brought closure to both of us because that incident
had changed both of our lives in a negative way. From that moment
forward I wanted all of my focus to be on getting back to the level
I was playing at before the injury and earning back my spot in the
starting lineup. The tackle was behind me.

A couple of days after my surgery, while I was in hospital in Colorado, a few of the Colorado Rapids players had visited me. Tyrone

Marshall and Sanna Nyassi, two former teammates of mine, had been in that group. I later found out that the player who had injured me also wanted to visit me in hospital but for some reason he wasn't able to come. I don't know if someone advised him against it or not, but I would have gladly allowed him to visit.

By now you've noticed that I have yet to call him by name. The reason for not using his name in this book is simple: the intent behind this book is to inspire people with my story of having to fight through a career-threatening injury, not to relive the tackle. It was a difficult moment for both him and me, and I don't want to permanently tie his name to that one tackle; his career was more than that. I had played against him several times before and there had never been a problem. The tackle was not personal or premeditated, it was just a horrible, dangerous tackle that has no place in the world of sports. But there was nothing personal behind it. I actually called him the night before the ten game suspension he received for injuring me was set to end. It was a phone call that took him by surprise, but it offered closure for both of us. I told him that I wished him the best, and that I would try to use my voice in the media to make it clear that I had moved on from the incident and so that there was no need for the fans to keep booing him.

After that Colorado game Sigi said to me, "Now that we've gotten that out of the way, I'm going to treat you like all of the other players. If you want to play major minutes, you'll have to earn them like everyone else. I know you have been through a lot, but I can't play you for any reason other than you deserving to play." I got the message loud and clear. Sigi had given me five minutes against Colorado to reward me for the work I had done thus far, but if I was going to get back into the team and be a contributor again I would have to earn my playing time.

For the next few weeks I didn't play in any games. I was usually on the bench but not once did I come on. That was a new experience for me as I had always been used to playing. It was humbling. Since my injury I had played in a few reserve team games and the five minutes against Colorado. I grew extremely frustrated during this period because I was not going to be able to get back to where I wanted to be unless I played in some games.

I was doing very well in training, I was feeling like my old self again, but for whatever reason when it came to games I was never selected. I knew that I wasn't quite at the pre-injury Steve Zakuani level yet, but I was close, and the only way to get all the way back there would be for me to play a few games in a row.

Things hit an all-time low when we went to Trinidad to play in a CONCACAF Champions League game. The Trinidadian team was not at the same level as any of the teams we played against in MLS every week, so I felt that it would be the perfect game for me to get some major minutes in as I worked my way back to one hundred percent fitness. We were leading by two or three goals in the second half when Sigi made his third and final substitution of the night. *But I've been playing really well in practice. If I can't get into a game that we're winning by two goals against a weak opposition, then I have no chance of ever playing again.* I felt a mixture of anger and frustration as I sat on the bench watching the game.

With about two minutes left in the game Sigi turned and looked at the bench. "Zakuani," he called, and motioned for me to come over to him. I got up from my seat and started walking toward him. I've never been able to hide my emotions, so I knew Sigi could see that I was pissed at him from a mile away. It was written all over my face. At the end of the day even though there are many factors that go into selecting a team, from the players view it's always the coach's decision regarding who plays and who doesn't, and since I hadn't been playing I blamed Sigi.

"Did you expect to play tonight?" he asked as he put his arm around me.

"Yeah" I replied. "I did."

"Well, the reason I didn't put you in tonight is because you have been playing really well in practice," he said, and then paused to watch the game for a few seconds. *Is this some kind of sick joke? I'm not playing in the game because I've been playing well in practice?* Sigi turned his attention back to our conversation and continued, "You've been playing really well in practice, so I didn't put you in tonight because you are going to start our next league game on Sunday in Dallas."

I was completely speechless as a huge smile came across my face. My frustration with Sigi evaporated into thin air as his words gave me one of the happiest moments of my career. A player's opinion of his or her coach is usually directly related to the amount of playing time they get!

I was going to start in the next game! I hadn't even been used as a sub in the last few weeks and now I was going to start the next game. This was great news. Sigi sensed my excitement and said, "That should make you feel good. You've earned it."

It was a Thursday night and we were going to fly directly from Trinidad to Dallas for our game on Sunday. Between Thursday and Sunday I slept no more than ten hours. I was too excited to sleep.

THE FIVE HUNDREDTH DAY

The Dallas game fell on September 2 2012. It was exactly five hundred days since my injury and since I had last started an MLS game. My main goal after my injury, the one that had driven me in all of my rehab work, had been to earn back my place in the starting lineup. I had challenged myself to overcome the five surgeries and get back into the Sounders' starting lineup. And now there I was, five hundred days later, accomplishing my goal. I felt a sense of pride and accomplishment as I put on my jersey and walked out of the tunnel and onto the field at Pizza Hut Park.

This moment was the one I had dreamed most about. It was the one moment I had prayed and sweated for. There had been days in my rehab when I'd felt that it was beyond my reach to ever start in an MLS game again. I'm talking about the days on which I hadn't made much progress in the gym and my bones ached from a hard practice. On those days, I had come so close to throwing in the towel and quitting. I had even thought of retiring a few months earlier. But on this hot day in Dallas I was glad that I hadn't. As I stood on the field waiting for the referee's whistle to get the game under way I was proud of myself for not quitting when all the odds had been against me.

During the game I wrote a message on the tape on my wrist. It simply said "500." It was one hundred degrees that day, and with this being my first start for the Sounders in over a year I knew that I would get tired very quickly. The message on my wrist was there to give me strength when I got tired. Whenever I was breathing hard and wanted to stop running I simply looked at my wrist—500—and I was instantly reminded of how long I had waited for this opportunity. That constant reminder gave me enough fuel to play sixty-five minutes and record a great assist to our captain, Mauro Rosales. A start and an assist—I'd missed this feeling!

I was standing out on the left wing when the ball made its way to me. I took a couple of touches before looking up and seeing a Dallas defender approaching me. Instinctively, I did what I have always done when faced with a one versus one situation; I pushed the ball into the open space and accelerated past the defender. For everyone watching in the stands and on TV this was definitely vintage Zakuani. As I raced towards the goal, I saw Rosales open at the back post so I crossed it right to him and he did the rest. I celebrated as if I was the one who'd scored. Five hundred days was a very long time for me to wait for this feeling – the gym work and rehab had paid off.

Every single one of my teammates congratulated me after the game. They had seen firsthand how hard I had worked to be able to be back out there with them and they wanted to let me know that this moment belonged to me. The coaching staff—Sigi, Brian, Ezra Hendrickson, Tom Dutra, Dave Tenney, and Kurt Schmid—all made it a point to congratulate me as well, as did Nolan Myer and Brett Johnson, our equipment guys. Randy and Chris, the two trainers who had tolerated my complaints during my rehab, both gave me a pat on the back. Before the game, as I was warming up, I had a brief conversation with Adrian and Chris Henderson, our technical director, and they'd both told me that getting back on the field after what I had been through was a big achievement. I slapped a high-five with Matt Gaschk from our media team and exchanged a hug with Grant Clarke, our team administrator, right before I left the locker room to board the team bus to the airport. The reason I'm listing all of these people is because I would have never been able to achieve my goal without all of the support I received from them. In the truest sense of the word it had been a team effort.

I rarely drink alcohol unless I am having a glass of wine with my dinner, but on this night I ordered a glass of champagne to my hotel room. I toasted to myself, I took a few sips, and then I slept like a baby. I'd been to hell and back in the last five hundred days, but in that moment I was very much in heaven as I celebrated my return to the pitch.

CHAPTER 8

THE THREE MOMENTS

One of my best performances in a Sounders jersey was actually after my injury. It was in the 2012 MLS Western Conference Final against the Los Angeles Galaxy. I'd spent most of the first leg watching from the bench as L.A. had beaten us 3-0. In order to advance to the MLS Cup we'd have to overturn the three-goal deficit in the second leg. We knew that it would take a superhuman effort, but I sensed that we were up for the challenge.

I was in the starting lineup for the second leg and I proceeded to give one of the best performances of my career. Even though football is a team game there are always different individual matchups from game to game. For this game I was up against Sean Franklin, who I consider to be the best right back I played against in my career. We'd had our fair share of battles over the years. I'd won some and lost others, but on this night I didn't give him a chance. After the game he told me that my performance was the best he had ever faced from a left-winger. It was one of those nights when everything that I tried came off.

We led L.A. 2-0 with thirty minutes to go and I fully expected us to go on and get the 4-0 win we needed, but they scored a penalty shortly after our second goal, which knocked the stuffing out of us, and the game finished 2-1. That night, because of my performance, was the first time since my injury that I truly felt I would be able to go on and be the dominant player I was on my way to becoming before the injury occurred.

I believe that after my leg break I was able to return to being ninety percent of the player I had been before the injury, which was more than enough to be a top player in MLS. From October 2012 to April 2013 I felt very much like my old self, and I played that way too.

However, in May 2013, two years after my broken leg, just when I was getting a run of games and beginning to rediscover my form, I tore my groin in practice.

I tore it as I attempted a play I had done a million times in my life. But for some reason, on that wet May morning in Seattle, my leg gave out and I heard a loud tear in my groin area. It was every bit as painful as it sounds. I had surgery in Philadelphia a few weeks later, and then I did rehab for a few months. I was able to overcome that groin injury, and by September I was feeling good and I was back in practice.

A few short weeks later, in mid-October, I tore my groin again after playing just fifteen minutes in a game against the Portland Timbers. I was devastated. I had been working hard in the gym to make sure my groin would be able to withstand the intensity of a game. I even took painkillers before every game to give me peace of mind more than anything, but once again, my body seemed to be unable to withstand any real intensity. As I walked off the field after that Portland game, I felt a burning sensation in my groin area and I immediately knew that once the adrenaline and painkillers wore off, I would be unable to walk pain-free, let alone play..

Two groin tears in five months, it was unbelievable. That second groin tear ruled me out for the rest of the 2013 season. I had another surgery in December, this time in Santa Monica, to try and repair my groin for a second time. It was those two groin injuries that happened so close together that would ultimately end my career. I did my best to fight back. I always do. But there would come a time when I knew I just simply had to stop fighting.

I entered the 2014 season with a lot of excitement and enthusiasm. Although I was coming off my second groin surgery in the space of a few months, I felt confident that I would be able to regain my former level. In the offseason I had signed with the Portland Timbers, bringing an end to my five-year stay in Seattle.

I spent the first few months of my time with Portland rehabbing my groin in the gym. In those months my spirit was always high, as I couldn't wait to start my new adventure. The Timbers' owner, Merritt Paulson, their GM, Gavin Wilkinson, and their entire coaching staff had made me feel very welcome as soon as I'd arrived in Portland. I had a lot of close friends on the team and within the organization, which had made my transition a very smooth one.

When I finally left the gym and joined the team in practice I began to show glimpses of my old self and within a few weeks of being back in practice I was named in the starting lineup. I expected my time with the Timbers to take off from that point on, but that never happened. I tore my hamstring twice in two months and my groin still didn't feel a hundred percent right, even though I had done everything in my power to try and fix it.

I worked extensively with Nik Wald, the Timbers' trainer, and Nick Milonas, the Timbers' fitness coach, as they put me through a routine that focused on getting my body to stop breaking down. I did a thousand different core strength exercises in the gym, I did acupuncture, I wore a heel lift in my boots to take stress off of my groin every time my foot hit the ground as I ran, and I even modified my practice schedule. Instead of spending five days out on the field with the rest of the team, I spent only three. On the other two days I was in the gym going through an exercise program that was tailored to meet my individual needs.

All of those approaches helped me and I was able to play in a few games and get through some hard practices, but ultimately they were short-term fixes for a bigger problem. The real issue was that my body had changed after undergoing seven surgeries in two and a half years, and no amount of acupuncture or weight lifting, was going to bring it back to how it used to be. That was a reality that I couldn't escape from, and when it hit me I knew that my days as a professional footballer were numbered.

When you are only twenty-six years old deciding to retire will never be an easy decision. It took me several months and a lot of tough conversations with myself before I was able to reach the point where I felt this was the right decision to make. I had to ask myself some really difficult but necessary questions that eventually made the decision slightly easier. I have received a thousand questions from people in the wake of my decision. I want to use this section of the book to answer a few of those.

Was there one moment that led you to this decision?

If I can be completely honest, I have to say that the idea of retirement first entered my mind on April 22, 2011, when my leg was broken and also during the summer of 2012 while I was still with Seattle. But as I fought back from that injury and eventually made it onto the pitch I stopped thinking about retirement and put all of my energy into rebuilding my career. Even when I suffered the two groin tears in 2013 my focus was only on getting myself back onto the field.

Signing for the Timbers was something that excited me because it was a new start and a chance to reinvent myself. I was looking forward to reconnecting with my college coach, Caleb Porter, and some former college teammates like Darlington Nagbe, Michael Nanchoff, and Ben Zemanski. I was especially excited about playing with Darlington because I have known him since he was sixteen and I've watched him become a top five player in MLS. I entered the season with great excitement, but after struggling to fully overcome my groin issues and struggling with a couple of hamstring tears I began to think about retirement again. There were three specific moments when I knew that I needed to retire.

The first was when I woke up one morning feeling like I had been run over by a train. I'd had a game the night before, and waking up sore the following day is completely normal, but this was different. I wasn't just feeling sore. I was in pain. Bending down to tie my shoes left me in agony. I avoided walking up the stairs because every time I lifted my legs it would hurt my groins. I asked myself a few questions, *Do you really want to keep feeling like this? What about when you have kids one day, how will you play with them if you can't even tie your shoes without pain? How much long term damage am I doing to my body?* Those questions planted the seed of me giving some serious thought to retiring.

The second moment was after a Champions League game in Guyana for the Timbers. The game had gone extremely well; we'd won 4-1 and I'd scored my first goal for the Timbers. But on the plane ride home, as I sat down and looked out of the window, I felt empty. I couldn't quite put my finger on what it was, but there was something missing. I wasn't sad or depressed, I was just empty. In that moment I realized that I no longer loved the game in the way I always had. Football had become about treatment tables, painkillers, MRIs, hospital visits, surgeries, and pain. The multiple injuries had taken their toll on me and had slowly drained the love of football from me. I got back to the U.S. and mentioned something to my fiancée, Ashley. It was the first time I had ever told someone that I no longer loved football.

The third moment was when I came across this Steve Jobs quote:

> "For the past thirty-three years, I have looked in the mirror every morning and asked myself: 'If today were the last day of my life, would I want to do what I am about to do today?' And whenever the answer has been 'No' for too many days in a row, I know I need to change something."

I read that quote and decided to apply it to my life. After four days of doing that I knew I was going to retire. In the morning when I woke up I didn't look forward to driving into practice. I used to love driving into work because it never actually felt like work, but during the experiment I realized that I was now viewing what I did every day as a job. It was no longer fun and I knew why. It was impossible to enjoy my career if I had to spend a few months out of every season recovering from surgery. On the fourth day, I had a conversation with my coach, Caleb Porter, and told him that I would most likely retire at the end of the season.

You're still so young and can play for ten more years. During that time isn't there a chance that you'd overcome your injuries once and for all?

That's a tough one to answer because I can't predict the future. I guess there was always a chance that given enough time my body would stop breaking down and I'd be able to complete a full season. However, the reality I have experienced every day for the past few years is that if I kept going I would eventually cause myself long-term damage. In the short term I could have taken pain meds and injections to help me get through the next few years, but the long-term risks of doing that were too great for me to choose that as a course of action.

Before announcing my decision to retire I took a break from football. I didn't go into training, I didn't work out in the gym, and I didn't attend any games. I avoided football completely. I did that because I wanted to see if I would miss driving into practice and being a part of a team, if I would miss the thrill of playing in front of thousands of screaming fans. After a few days away I realized that although I did miss it in some ways, the honest truth was that I didn't miss it enough to change my mind.

I enjoyed waking up pain free. I was able to go about my life without having to worry about the next doctor's appointment or the next MRI scan I'd have to have. During my break I took no painkillers and had no injections. I stopped putting my body through the stress it had been under. After a week of resting at home my body felt better than it had in a very long time. It's as if all of the pain I 'd been feeling had been my body's way of screaming at me, telling me to stop, and now that I was finally listening I was no longer in pain because my body no longer needed to scream.

Another thing that made me know it was the right time was the fact that I didn't want to be a player who just took up space on the roster. If I was a part of a team I wanted them to be able to count on me to help them be successful. My body hadn't allowed me to do that in the past few years, and so it was time to move on.

What will you do with your life now that you have stopped playing?

Earlier in the book I talked about how most professional athletes hate the thought of retirement. Athletes are scared to think about retirement because playing their sport is all they have ever known. Retirement throws you into the unknown; there's no security of a job or a paycheck once you decide that you are going to retire. For some reason I don't have those fears.

I once did, about three years ago when I first got injured, but now I'm not worried because I've had enough time to prepare myself for the next phase of my life. I have a few ideas about what I want to do over the next few years. Allow me to share some of them with you.

First off, I am not completely retiring from football. I am retiring from the playing aspect, but I'll remain involved in the game in other capacities, one of which is coaching. After playing the game for twenty-one years, six of them professionally, I feel that I have a lot to teach in regard to what it takes to become a professional footballer, both physically and mentally, so I'll definitely be setting up my own coaching business in the near future and offering my services to those who are interested. I'll be coaching individuals rather than teams. My desire is to work with a small group of players—one, two, three, four, or five at a time—and help them over the course of a few weeks or months to improve the areas of their game that they want help with. I could never just completely walk away from football and doing some individual coaching will be one way that I'll stay connected to the game.

Another thing I'll be doing is a lot more public speaking. Most people are afraid of public speaking, and I completely understand why, but for some reason I love it. I enjoy being in front of a group and sharing my story—my successes and failures—and my ideas on leadership, teamwork, and goal setting in the hopes of inspiring them to achieve the dreams they have. I view public speaking as an art form, like music.

Musicians have been connecting with people and inspiring them with their words for as long as we can remember, and I think that speaking has that same power of being a tool that can inspire people through the use of words. I was able to do quite a bit of public speaking during my career, but I usually had to turn down opportunities because of my schedule. I'll now be able to devote a huge part of my time to this passion, and I'm excited to meet people and share my story.

There are other things I'll be doing, like writing more books on some of the subjects I like speaking about and running my organization, Kingdom Hope, full time. We can never fully predict what the future holds for us but I am looking forward to living out some of my other dreams and passions. If I am half as successful in them as I was in pursuing my dream of being a footballer, I'll be very happy.

CHAPTER 9
KINGDOM HOPE

When I first arrived in Seattle back in January 2009 I had only one goal in mind and that was to be successful on the pitch for the Sounders. My dream was to do well for the Sounders and become one of the best players in MLS. I didn't give much thought to anything outside of football because my life at that time consisted of football and not much else. I didn't plan on accomplishing anything outside of football while I was still playing because I figured I would have all the time in the world to give back and reach my non-football goals after my career was over. Accomplish my football goals first, and then after my career I would get busy doing other stuff off the field—that was my plan.

But as soon as I met James Riley my plans changed. James was one of the first teammates I became good friends with off the field. He was a bit older (okay, a lot older, sorry James!) than I was, he had been in the league for a while, and his warm personality made him a popular figure in the locker room. We both lived in downtown Seattle, and since I didn't have a car when I first arrived in Washington, James would pick me up and we would carpool to training every day. It was on one of those morning drives to training that James introduced me to a perspective that was different from the one I had. As we pulled up to Starfire, our practice facility, James turned to me and said, "Hey, just want to give you a heads up. After practice I'm not going to go straight home. I need to make a stop at the Boys and Girls Club so I can spend some time with the kids."

"The boys and who?" I replied in confusion.

"The Boys and Girls Club. If you come with me, you'll see what they're about."

That was the first time I had ever heard of the Boys and Girls Club, but it would definitely not be the last. James, I would come to learn, was extremely active in the community. On top of all the community work that we did through the Sounders, he did a lot of his own work on the side with local charities and foundations, especially those that catered to kids. He spent a lot of his spare time giving back in ways I had never even thought of.

That afternoon, after training, I went with James to the Boys and Girls Club and had the time of my life. I lost track of time as I ran around chasing the kids and helping them with their schoolwork. I answered all of the questions they had for me, "How big is your house? How fast can you run? What's your favorite color? Are you faster than Superman?" There was no end to their curiosity. The questions were not a one-way street, though, because I took the time to ask them my own set of questions. One thing I've learned in life is that the fastest way to show someone that you are interested in learning about them is to ask them questions. And so over the years whenever I've been around people who are asking me a lot of questions I return the favor and ask them questions so that they can tell me about themselves. I've learned a lot of interesting things about people that way.

That afternoon spent at the Boys and Girls club re-lit a spark inside me that had been dormant for a while. Ever since I had heard Myles Munroe speak and I began reading his books I knew that before I died I wanted to help as many people as I could to become the best they could be. I wasn't entirely sure how I would do it, but I just knew that I had the desire to do it. Myles Munroe had taught me that true leadership was a result of serving other people.

My athletic gift had given me a magnificent platform from which I could serve many people in many ways. However, I had always planned to act on that desire to serve people after I finished my playing career, not during it. That changed after my trip to the Boys and Girls Club. Those kids made such an impression on me that within a year of meeting them I had established my own organization called Kingdom Hope. The big idea behind Kingdom Hope was to have it as the vehicle I could use to create a variety of programs that would inspire people to realize their dreams. My dream was to hold football clinics in the greater Seattle area so that I could teach some football skills to the kids and adults who attended. Kingdom Hope held several clinics during my time in Seattle and they were always well attended and successful.

Another thing I wanted to do was to teach and share the life lessons I had learned from Mr. Goodison Goodison, Myles Munroe, and
the hundreds of books I had read. I wanted to do for others what
Myles Munroe had done for me. I wanted to use my words to motivate
and inspire others to do more and be more. That's how my interest
in public speaking began. Between 2010 and 2013 I spoke at several events in many different settings and to many different types of
people. I spoke in churches, to business leaders, to student athletes
and regular students, to rotary clubs, and to disadvantaged youth. My
goal in every single talk was to spark something in people that would
help them to fulfill their potential. I spoke on how to set goals and
reach them, what it means to be a leader, how to maximize your potential, and how to work with a team.

Establishing Kingdom Hope really allowed me to tap into my passion to serve people, and I hope to continue to do that in the years to
come, hopefully on an even bigger scale than what I have been able to
do so far.

After James took me to the Boys and Girls Club I began to do a
lot of charity work. I donated my time and money to charities, I visited a couple of hospitals, I began going to the Boys and Girls Club
in my own time, and I was a constant fixture at many schools across
Washington. From elementary schools to high schools, I visited them
all. James taught me the value of being active in the community and
giving back, and it's a lesson I will never forget or neglect.

After that first trip to the Boys and Girls Club I began planting the
seeds for what I wanted to do with my life after my football career was
over. It's a good thing I did that, because as I was about to find out a
sports career can be an extremely fragile thing.

Although it was officially founded in 2010, Kingdom Hope has existed
in my mind since 2006. My dream behind Kingdom Hope was to provide programs that would help people to maximize their potential as
human beings. It was a simple dream. As I matured and wrote down
my plans the dream began to take shape and I surrounded myself with
a great team that has helped me bring this dream to fruition.

Currently Kingdom Hope runs soccer clinics, soccer camps, and
leadership seminars. In the near future we will be launching The Cecile
Zakuani Scholarship, named after my mom, in partnership with These

Numbers Have Faces, an organization based in Portland, Oregon. The idea is to financially aid a few African students each year to attend university, primarily in Rwanda, and mentor them as they use their education to make a difference in their continent.

My ultimate dream with Kingdom Hope, however, is to establish a football academy in London. I have too many talented friends who never became footballers because they were taken in by the street life, and I want to play my part in making sure that the streets doesn't rob the world of any more talented potential footballers. There were two things that saved me from going in the same direction as some of my friends: Myles Munroe's teachings and Abbey's team.

While my friends sold drugs, I read books all day, and then in the evening I played with Abbey's team. I want to take my experience and make it available to several kids at a time.

The academy will function like a boarding school and will be fully equipped with state-of-the-art practice facilities and dorms. I want it to be a place that kids want to come and be a part of. When a kid finishes school at sixteen, if he hasn't received a professional contract, rather than give up on his dreams like so many do he can attend Kingdom Hope Football Academy and go through our two-year program, which consists of formal education, leadership training, daily football practice, and a weekly game. I literally want to take the transformative experience that I had at sixteen and make it available to a lot of teenagers in the future.

After their two-year stay at our academy we will send all of their highlight tapes to colleges and pro teams (like Abbey did for me), giving them the opportunity to pursue a career in professional or collegiate soccer. That's my ultimate dream: to help young boys who find themselves in the same position I was in when I was their age become better leaders and maybe professional footballers.

As I work toward that ultimate goal of establishing the football academy I'm enjoying being a part of all the current programs that Kingdom Hope is running. If you would like to know more about what Kingdom Hope does and how you can benefit from our programs or get involved, visit our website, www.kingdom-hope.org, or visit my site, www.stevezakuani.com.

CHAPTER 10
KEEP ON KEEPING ON

This is my word of encouragement to anyone who has ever known tremendous hardship and felt like quitting: I've been in your shoes.

The past three years of my life can only be described as the biggest test of character I have ever faced. There's a famous Bob Marley quote that says, "You will never know how strong you are, until being strong is your only choice." That statement has been my experience for the past three years. Two broken bones, two groin tears, two hamstring tears, seven surgeries, twenty-six of the last thirty-six months spent rehabbing from various injuries, and having to retire in my mid-twenties is enough to make anyone lie down and give up. But as I went through each new challenge I kept telling myself that I was stronger than what I was facing.

At first I had a hard time believing myself when I said that, but over time the more I repeated it the more that mindset became ingrained in me. I am stronger than what I am facing. You have to believe that about yourself. Every time I suffered an injury I knew that I would be spending the next few months on the treatment table. I knew that I would have injections and surgeries and that I would have to dig really deep within myself if I ever wanted to play again. But I also knew that I had what it would take to come back from anything and that the worst thing I could do was to lose hope. When you feel like quitting: don't.

If your pain is overwhelming and you feel like crying, then cry. If you want to just vent to yourself sometimes, then go ahead and vent. But whatever you do, don't ever give up. I came close to giving up so many times, but I kept fighting back because I knew that I was inspiring people. Young kids write to me all the time and tell me that I am their favorite player. I know they're watching my every move, and I know that one day they will face adversity in their own lives. When that day of adversity comes to them, I want them to be able to look at me and draw strength from my story. *Steve didn't quit, and neither will I.* That's why you should never quit: you never know who you are inspiring just by holding on.

When I decided to retire I did so only after giving everything I had in my fight to get back on the field. The fact that I fought back and played in some games after every single surgery I had is proof that I fought through my trials with everything I have. When it became clear to me that to keep fighting would mean having to put my body on the line in ways that could have dire long-term consequences I knew it was time to stop fighting. It was time to dust myself off and leave the game behind with my head held high. There's a difference between giving up and knowing when it's time to stop fighting. My encouragement to those facing adversity is to keep fighting back with everything you have, keep fighting and never give in. And once you have fought back with every fiber of your being, allow the outcome to be what it will. If things don't turn out for the best, at least you can sleep knowing that you gave it your all and then some. You can't control how things turn out, you can only control whether you will fight or give up.

One of my roommates in college used to always tell me, "Steve, sometimes, you just have to keep on keeping on." What he meant was that when life seems hard and you've been knocked down more times than you can count you have to pick yourself back up and just keep going. As someone who has known his fair share of suffering, I encourage you to do what I always to try do when life knocks me down. I just keep on keeping on.

There's life on the other side of your storm,

~ Steve

ABOUT THE AUTHOR

Steve Zakuani was born in the Democratic Republic of Congo, moving to London when he was four years old. His soccer career started early in life playing for the Arsenal youth academy in London, and then attending the University of Akron on a soccer scholarship. Zakuani's professional career began when the Seattle Sounders drafted him with the first pick of the 2009 MLS SuperDraft. He was a finalist for MLS Rookie of the Year in 2009, and in 2010 he was the joint-leading scorer for the Sounders with 10 goals. In the 2010 MLS postseason he scored the Sounders first ever MLS Playoff goal.

In 2014, Zakuani signed with the Portland Timbers but his time at the club was limited to just one season due to injuries.

In total, Zakuani played six seasons as a professional, amassing over 100 appearances but he will be the first to admit that a series of injuries severely limited what he could have achieved on the field.

Steve founded Kingdom Hope in 2010, to share his story of overcoming the adversities that accompany growing up in a low-income neighborhood of London. Through the help of various mentors in his life, Steve was able to realize his potential and achieve his dreams of becoming a professional soccer player. Kingdom Hope offers programs designed to help people fulfill their dreams and find success in life.